About the Author

John Phillips was born in Yorkshire and grew up in Wimbledon, attending King's College School and Oxford University.

He was a foreign reporter for UPI and *The Times*. He is editor of *The Italian Insider*.

WHITE EAGLE
OVER WIMBLEDON

Also by John Phillips

Macedonia: Warlords and rebels in the Balkans

Algeria: Anger of the dispossessed (with Martin Evans)

WHITE EAGLE
OVER WIMBLEDON

How Poland's war affected a London Childhood

JOHN PHILLIPS

Copyright © John Phillips 2017

First printed in this edition 2017

Insider Press
Via dell'Umiltà 83c,
Rome 00187
Italy
info@italianinsider.it

The right of John Phillips to be identified as the author of this work has been asserted by him in accordance with the Copyright, Designs and Patents Act, 1988.

All rights reserved. No part of this publication may be reproduced, stored in a retrieval system, or transmitted, in any form, or by any means, electronic, mechanical, photocopying, recording or otherwise, without the prior permission of the publishers.

This book is sold subject to the condition that it shall not, by way of trade or otherwise, be lent, resold, hired out, or otherwise circulated without the author's prior consent in any form of binding or cover other than that in which it is published and without a similar condition being imposed on the subsequent purchaser. Requests to publish work from this book must be sent to John Phillips, via email at jhghill@yahoo.com.

ISBN: 978-1-5272106-2-2

Cover design: Margaux Phillips

V1.1

Contents

Preface	i
Chapter 1: For King, bed and breakfast	1
Chapter 2: Half eagle, half lion	15
Chapter 3: Brazilian interlude	32
Chapter 4: Double patriotism	40
Chapter 5: Rough, tough and desperately unjust	56
Chapter 6: I am listening	63
Chapter 7: Roundheads and Cavaliers	84
Chapter 8: The Universal Blow	109
Chapter 9: Poles of perception	117
Chapter 10: The Castle	132
Chapter 11: Tidying up history	148
Chapter 12: We always go back	170
Chapter 13: 'Cowards: fire lower'	184
Chapter 14: 'Working for the Secret Service'	194
Chapter 15: Down and Out	204
Chapter 16: A little sex, no sex	210
Chapter 17: Return to Lubartow	219
Acknowledgements	241
Notes	243

Photo credits

Cover photo: Ireneusz Filipowicz, exhausted conscript of Polish people's army during 'liberation' of Warsaw. — Phillips family collection

Photo of author — Charlotte Smeds

Caption	Credit
The author as a young man with 'Uncle John'	Andrzej Filipowicz
Jan Filipowicz, the young Polish Air Force officer…	Andrzej Filipowicz
Ireneusz Filipowicz, in Polish cadet uniform.	Phillips family collection
Our Wimbledon home after a rare snowfall.	Diana Phillips
Mum in the Army, circa 1949	Ruth Gee
Me and Dad	Phillips family collection
Gryf' in Warsaw as a conscript of the Polish 'people's army.'	Phillips family collection
Dad, in Polish 2nd Corps after defecting to West, with Warsaw Uprising anchor badge on battledress.	Phillips family collection
Artillery training with Polish free forces in Italy.	Phillips family collection
Dad on patrol in Italy	Phillips family collection
Student days, Dundee.	Andrzej Filipowicz
Dad's 12th Polish Artillery regiment identity card.	Phillips family collection
Family reception for my parents' wedding vow renewal...	Phillips family collection
Sketch of Anna De Laveaux…	Imperial War Museum
Me at work in the Wimbledon Guardian office, 1980.	John Phillips
Me working for UPI, Spanish Steps, Rome	Carlo di Renzo
Me on assignment in Sarajevo…	Leandro Turriani
Identity card issued to me by Druze PSP party…	John Phillips
Reporting the 2001 Macedonian small war.	Kristian Kahrs
The Times office, Belgrade, 2003	Dragan Petrovic
Andrzej Filipowicz	Teresa Filipowicz

*For Diana, Andrzej and
"Uncle John," Flying Officer Jan Filipowicz.*

Preface

It is sad to record that fear and resentment of Polish immigrants evidently inspired many xenophobic Britons to vote for Brexit in 2016.

In August 2016 Arek Jozwik, a 40-year-old Polish factory worker, was murdered by a gang of teenage English schoolchildren who punched him to the ground in Harlow after they heard him speaking Polish. On a bus in Newcastle a boy set a Polish woman's hair on fire and there was estimated to be a 41 percent surge in hate crimes in the UK the month after the Brexit vote, many of them against Poles.

Yet as recently as three generations ago as many as 200,000 Poles who had fought the Nazis as Britain's 'first ally' were welcomed to the UK.

When I began writing this memoir a decade ago, hundreds of thousands of Poles already had come to work in Britain following Poland's membership of the EU in 2004. But their presence had not yet generated the hostility that later was whipped up by UKIP and further-right parties.

In 2014 UKIP won the 2014 European elections on the issue of EU immigrant labour, One infamous poster read: "26 million people in Europe are looking for work, and whose jobs are they after?"

In fact this was not the first time that an influx of Poles to Britain fuelled hostility. There was a wave of anti-Polish sentiment in the British labour movement in the late 1940s and, as we shall see, British authorities treated Polish political refugees in the 1950s as 'aliens' who were placed under close surveillance for years before they could become 'naturalised' UK citizens.

Nevertheless such suspicion and hostility at the time was not on the scale of the recent incidents in which in the popular English mind, in the provinces of the North in particular, all East Europeans, be they Lithuanians, Ukrainians, Latvians, Bulgarians or Rumanians often are grouped together as 'Poles.' The old Polish Commonwealth including the Baltic States and Ukraine bizarrely has been resuscitated in a dark part of the popular English mind.

Dagmar Rita Myślińska, a prescient Lecturer at the University at Albany, New York, has explored how "the Brexit debate reinforced a climate of antagonism towards Poles and other Central-Eastern Europeans. But the expression of such attitudes with impunity has been a part of the political and media discourse long before the referendum." [1]

White Eagle Over Wimbledon

Ms Myślińska, a Ph.D student at the London School of Economics, found that the post-Brexit wave of hate crimes against Poles, in particular, "has brought to the foreground the dangers of accepting prejudices and racism as a normalised part of discourse, while revealing some insights about the nature of white ethnic and national identity in the UK."

"Poles have been perceived as second-class European citizens and targeted as scapegoats by some right-wing politicians, the media, and the public since before the time of Poland's accession to the EU in 2004," she said.

"Poles' experiences in the UK have been complicated by their whiteness. Although being white can help Poles to find employment opportunities and to be less visible as an outsider group in the UK, it can also make expressions of prejudice against them more culturally acceptable than they would be against non-white groups."

This book recounts the history of one family, part of the thriving Anglo-Polish community in London in the 1960s and 1970s, which integrated into a gentler English society after my father arrived in Britain as a political refugee at the end of an odyssey that took him from Poland to Germany and Italy as a young Polish soldier. Then, as now, Polish business men and women made a dynamic contribution to the British economy and Polish servicemen's gallant contribution to the Allied cause was still a vivid memory.

John Phillips

The Poles and the British could be said to have enjoyed a love-hate relationship over the past 75 years. It is hoped that any insights from this book can help to strengthen and reinforce the two peoples' long friendship in the future so that love may prevail.

John Phillips
Rome, July 2017

Chapter 1:
For King, bed and breakfast

"The bloody Brits," Uncle Jan yelled. "They let us down." With those words, the big Polish airman crash landed on the shiny polished parquet floor of the hall of our house in Wimbledon.

A tall, cadaverous man always dressed immaculately in a grey suit and tie, Uncle John, as we called him, was a former Polish Air Force flier who had been a regular officer since 1930, when he was 22.

One of the more colourful visitors to our home, my great uncle was of keen interest to a small boy. In family legend we children had built him up as a war hero, a dashing "Squadron leader in the battle of Britain."

The truth was different, but perhaps no less interesting for that. When he launched into his attack on the British, Uncle and his Scottish wife, Aunt Jessie, had been staying with us on a visit from their home in the North while my father was away on business.

John Phillips

Uncle John was a little in his cups that morning after plundering the drinks cabinet in an old Japanese style lacquer gramophone cabinet in our living room looking onto the long back garden of the house on Belvedere Drive. His frustration about the fate of Poland during the Second World War still rankled in the 1960s.

"Churchill promised us more planes but they never came," he continued, "We were left to fight alone."

I was flattered by his avuncular attention on such soldierly matters. My worldly and somewhat bonkers uncle evidently considered an 11-year-old schoolboy not entirely "a bloody Brit," but by implication at least, Polish, someone who should know the truth about a perfidious betrayal.

The enchanting spell was broken, however, when Uncle John's tirade ended almost as abruptly as it erupted.

Dr Kelly, the family doctor, a resourceful New Zealand lady of about the same vintage as Aunt Jessie, raced over from her Morden road surgery in her Morris Minor. Without wasting time to take off her purple hat and cream lambswool coat, she jabbed the comatose Uncle with what we were told was a morphine injection to calm him down.

"I have had as much as I can take," long-suffering Jessie shrugged in broad Glaswegian at the end of the drama. Uncle and Aunt slipped away to the guest room at the back of the house, leaving early for their home in the north the next day at dawn.

White Eagle Over Wimbledon

Uncle may have been considered in disgrace but his insistence on the notion that all had not gone well in the War, contrary to the vision propounded by patriotic comics I read such as The Victor, intrigued me.

In our music lessons at my school by Wimbledon Common, we sang Rule Britannia, vowing that "Britons never, never, never will be slaves." Nevertheless, it seemed that Britain might have allowed her first allies to remain slaves.

The author as a young man with 'Uncle John'

When Dad came home, he weighed in to England's defence, setting the record straight. Uncle John had got it wrong, he said, Britain had done its best for the fractious Poles.

"Winston Churchill always behaved decently," he told me, "he did what he could for the Poles."

Sir Winston Churchill had obtained approval from Parliament for all the Poles in Britain who had been officers and didn't want to return to Poland under Communism to be offered British citizenship and a university education.

In 1944, in fact, Churchill asked Anthony Eden, the foreign secretary, to "reassure these men who have fought in the Polish Divisions that whatever else happens to them, the British Empire will find them a home." [2]

The great man thought of the Poles again during the Yalta debate in 1945, when he made his "pledge" to the Poles:

"In any event. His Majesty's Government will never forget the debt they owe to the Polish troops who served them so valiantly, and to all those who have fought under our command," Churchill said.

"I earnestly hope it may be possible to offer the citizenship and freedom of the British Empire, if they so desire ... we should think it an honour to have such faithful and valiant warriors dwelling among us as if they were men of our own blood."

Dad added that Polish inter-war leaders had brought some woes on the country by inveterate squabbling with their neighbours, the Czechs, other allies who became alienated when Poland in 1938 ungraciously grabbed a chunk of Czech territory.

Against this background the demon drink had sabotaged Uncle John's career in the RAF, Dad added. "He had arguments with his superiors. Eventually he was grounded."

As my father's only relative in England when he arrived in Britain after he left the Army, "Uncle John was a disappointment," Dad said.

White Eagle Over Wimbledon

"He wouldn't get drunk every day, but every now and again he would go out and come back completely pissed."

Uncle John's past remained a mystery for me until 50 years later when I obtained his service record from the RAF. A member of No. 4 Polish Air Force Regiment based at Toruń, Jan Filipowicz had trained as a navigator at the Polish Air Force officers' academy at Deblin. In the 1930s the Air Force was an élite though alcoholism was rife and disputes between officers still were settled with duels.

Jan Filipowicz, the young Polish Air Force officer, with navigator's eagle badge.

One duel in Uncle's regiment was recalled by a historian. "In 1928, when two officers of the 4 Toruń Air Regiment had a minor disagreement, the regimental commander himself sent a plane to Warsaw to pick up a pair of duelling pistols so that they could resolve it." [3]

"In 40 percent of cases the duels ended without a scratch, honour having been satisfied by the mere discharge of pistols, but a staggering 25 percent ended fatally."

Uncle Jan survived his decade of peacetime service without becoming a fatal statistic. He took part in the campaign in Poland after the German invasion, from Sept. 1 to Sept. 21, 1939.

As Polish forces were overrun by the Nazis, Air Force officers were ordered to leave the country to resume the fight abroad. Uncle crossed the Polish-Hungarian frontier on Sept. 22 with men under his command. He was interned in Hungary until Nov. 1, then made his way to France via Belgrade, Athens and Marseille where he joined the Polish forces in Lyon under British command.

Few records of the Polish Air Force's fight in France survive but Patrick Bishop, writing about 'Bomber boys' noted the pressure navigators worked under. "The pilot's concern was to reach the target. The navigator's job was to find it ... as a group they tended more to seriousness than the men they flew with."

"The job, and the training it required, were demanding and exhausting ... Astronavigation required an ability to think in three dimensions ... In the early days navigators had no radio aids to guide them to targets."

White Eagle Over Wimbledon

"... the navigator's job was the most mentally testing of aircrew tasks, requiring constant alertness at every stage of the journey." [4]

After the fall of France, Uncle was evacuated to the United Kingdom by ship, arriving June 26, 1940. He was one of the luckier Polish servicemen. Only 19,000 out of 80,000 Polish servicemen were able to escape to England from France.

Uncle joined the Polish Air Force formed under British command six weeks later, based initially with the Polish Air Force depot at Blackpool before being posted to No. 50 Operational Training Unit at RAF Aston Down in Gloucestershire.

Regular Polish Air Force officers like Uncle had difficulty adapting to the British system. He also may have been a casualty of Machiavellian politics within the Polish military.

After doing the six week observer course at Aston Down he was posted to the Polish Army Camp at Taighnabruaich in a remote part of Scotland.

This was an internment camp for Poles who opposed Gen. Sikorski, the Polish Prime Minister. Later its existence would be played up by the Communist authorities in Poland with official media terming it a concentration camp.

By October 1941 Uncle John was back in Blackpool before six months of postings to the Air Crew Training

Centre at RAF Hucknall in Nottinghamshire, the Initial Training Wing at Torquay and No 1 Elementary Air Observer School at RAF Eastbourne.

In all he spent five spells at Blackpool, with a further period at no 5 Air Observer School at RAF Jurby on the Isle of Man.

The following year, barely two years after arriving from France, he was placed on "extended leave" that lasted from July 15, 1942 to August 18, 1947.

Earlier in 1942 navigators from the Operational Training Units were used to make up the numbers in three "One thousand bomber raids" on Germany each involving some 1000 aircraft.

Bomber Command only had some 600 operational bombers so the others were obtained by using air crew who were not fully trained or who were scrounged from Coastal Command. Bomber Harris's idea was that German city defences would be overwhelmed by saturation bombing by 1000 aeroplanes attacking within 90 minutes.

On the night of May 30, 1942, as many as 890 bombers reached Cologne. The bombing did not create a general firestorm, as in Lübeck, but it did cause massive damage. According to German figures, 469 people were killed and 45,000 made homeless. "Only" 41 aircraft were lost. In all 367 training aircraft were used. Casualties among them were 11 percent compared to an average 2 percent.

White Eagle Over Wimbledon

Harris followed through with a second raid two nights later, deploying 956 bombers against industrial Essen. A third raid, in which 960 bombers targeted the coastal town of Bremen, took place June 25.

Another document in Uncle John's file, filled in by himself in his hand, noted the results of a medical board at 10 A.C.M.B. describing him as "Fit Pilot, Fit Observer." Another board in October 1941 remarked "fit Wireless Operator ... Fit Observer (Radio)."

However by the end of 1942 he was "released from service with the PAF and sent to Rothesay" for what he described without elaborating as "Disciplinary Reasons."

A dark section written in one of the most authoritative books about the Polish Air Force may have applied to Uncle.

"Blackpool was also where those who had been thrown out of squadrons were sent, so it was where the least desirable elements in the force naturally ended up. There was a hard core of difficult cases, whose motto was 'For King, Bed and Breakfast.' Some of the men, finding their experience too much for them, had cracked under the strain or giving way to depression."

"The Polish Air Force intelligence unit kept an eye on the situation," Adam Zamoyski added, "its reports often quote from letters written by demoralized airmen."

"'I don't bother thinking about things any more, Joe, because I'm sure that we won't go back to Poland anyway

...' one wrote to a colleague. 'I just drink, fuck and enjoy myself.'

The exact nature of the "disciplinary reasons" for Uncle's treatment were not stated. Polish navigators often chafed under the command of British pilots because "under Polish regulations the captain of the crew and therefore of the whole aircraft, including the passengers, was always the navigator, whereas under British regulations it was the pilot."

"The Polish Air Force in Great Britain came under the authority of the RAF and was therefore subject to British regulations." [5]

The RAF Polish Enquiries Section was unable to tell me whether Uncle took part in any active service. "Perhaps at the Operational Training Unit," the lady said.

"He was not the only one to have problems adapting to the British system," she said.

"There were a number who were insubordinate, because of the different training and because they had lost their country." [6]

A study of Poland's Government in exile confirmed that Taighnabruaich and another camp on the Isle of Bute off south Western Scotland were used by Sikorski to intern officers who were political opponents.

Bute was known as "the Isle of Serpents," and was considered a "penal settlement." Evan Mcgilvray considered

White Eagle Over Wimbledon

the internment on British soil of Poles "tarnished the Government-in-exile's credentials." [7]

Uncle John's bitter remarks to me 20 years later suggest that he may have been interned as part of a purge by Sikorski of officers who supported his arch-rival, Gen. Kazimierz Sosnowski.

In 1944 Sosnowski was dismissed as head of Polish armed forces after an outburst accusing the British Government of betraying Poland. Churchill mocked him as "General Sozzle-something."

But Sosnowski was respected by commanders such as Lieut. Gen. Carton de Wiart, the head of the British Military Mission in Poland in 1939, widely considered "more Polish than the Polish." He noted Sosnowski masterminded the battle of Lwow, the only Polish victory of the 1939 campaign against the Germans. [8]

At any rate Uncle's service was judged officially "satisfactory" in 1945. He was awarded the War Medal 1939-45 with its image of the King and, on the reverse, a lion standing on a double-headed dragon, signifying the enemy.

Under the Polish Resettlement Act a Polish soldier or sailor could join the Polish Resettlement Corps for two years. The Polish Air Force had their own PRC wing though Uncle John seems to have been slotted in with the army – not difficult given that all regular inter-war Polish air force officers spent two years doing regular army training before learning to fly.

Once a man was in the Resettlement corps he would carry out vocational training and take English classes whilst looking out for employment. When he found work he would be put on the "Class W (T) Reserve" list and continue to work out the days towards the two year mark when he would be a full fledged civilian.

The whole process was to act as a cushion for the Poles between the order of military life and the freedom of being a civilian, albeit in a new, foreign country.

Like many Polish servicemen Uncle John wound up finding humble employment in the UK, working as a "pressure polisher" for a Birmingham company.

It likely was a humiliating job after the glamour and excitement of being an aviator and perhaps coming down in the world fuelled rancour. Despite Dad's defence of Britain's record on Poland, however, a lingering suspicion remained in my mind that uncle had spoken some truth in his cups.

I found some resonance in the autobiography of philanthropist Sue Ryder, who worked with Polish agents sent to Poland by SOE and became "Baroness of Warsaw" in the House of Lords.

In 1939 "we talked about the courage of the Poles and their resistance and how remarkable the cavalry were to

White Eagle Over Wimbledon

fight on horseback against the German tanks," she said. "We expressed indignation at our inability to help them and the knowledge that we and the French had let down their country and our common cause." [9]

Some years later as the gas fire sputtered in our cosy lounge and the rain poured down on Wimbledon Common, Mum and I watched Randolph Churchill on the BBC defend his father from controversy aroused by Rolf Hochhuth's play The Soldiers

This insinuated Winston Churchill connived to murder Sikorski. The play spawned a vast literature about how Sikorski's fatal plane crash off Gibralter in 1942 may have been murder.

This included speculation that the Polish woman spy Christine Granville, and her friend Countess Teresa Lubienska, were murdered because of what they knew about Sikorski's end.

Granville, the model for Ian Fleming's Vesper Lynd in Casino Royale, was stabbed in the Shelbourne Hotel in Kensington in 1952. An Irishman, George Muldonway, a hanger-on who became a stalker, was hanged for the murder.

Countess Lubienska, aged 72, an Auschwitz and Ravensbruck survivor, was fatally stabbed on the staircase of Gloucester Road underground station in 1957. The killer ran off and never was found.

Programmes and films about Poland and the Second World War were broadcast sporadically on our black and white, single channel television, usually raising more questions for me than they solved unlike more popular, stirring epics of British daring-do with which the BBC spoon-fed our generation, such as The Dambusters or The Guns of Navarone.

Among the more unusual films I recall Mum and I seeing together was Kanal, Andrzej Wajda's film about the Warsaw Uprising of 1944.

I was perturbed by the stark scenes of young, wounded Home Army fighters trying to escape through the sewers as some of them went mad and Russian troops remained impassive on the other side of the Vistula, leaving their supposed Allies to be massacred by the Nazis.

The brilliant film immortalised what came to be seen as the first battle of the Cold War.

I had no inkling of how Dad had come to England after fighting in it and then, a year later, blazing a trail of freedom as a young defector deserting from the Red Army to escape to the West.

Chapter 2:
Half eagle, half lion

To try and learn more about my father's romantic world I poured myself a half tumbler of the 98 degree proof vodka from the flask he kept at the top of the breakfast room cupboard.

The impact of the powerful libation, knocked back in one at the tender age of 10, was tremendous. As my head swam and the room rotated I thought I might be going to die. Suddenly I had jumped back two generations into Uncle John's world.

I did not puke – the vodka was clean stuff though its strong peculiar smell was nauseous – but I realised I had made a terrible mistake by imbibing a dangerous adult potion. I staggered back to my bedroom.

In a similar spirit of adventure when I was five I filched two Players' untipped from Dad's cigarette box, tearing open one and stuffing it in a plastic bubble pipe to smoke.

Drinking with Dad thereafter was limited to the occasional glasses of Woodpecker cider he poured to wash down our "iron rations" of Polish sausage sandwiches and pickled cucumber on hot afternoons.

On such summer days my father planted and watered fir trees in our large, rambling garden behind our house in Belvedere Drive, recalling for him the lush forests of Poland.

Together, mixing the cement in a wheelbarrow, Dad and I built and painted white the high wall enclosing the front garden with its rose bushes and car port. The wall collapsed within hours on our first attempt. But the blocks were rock steady after we made a second effort with stronger cement that we mixed the next day on the pavement.

The three storey building with panoramic views was a wreck when we bought it.

It was one of the detached houses that was built after the Earl Spencer family sold their estate of Wimbledon Park in the 1840s as building land and a period of residential development began.

After it was re-wired, pointed and decorated we moved over from our old house two miles away in Conway Road, a quiet street lined with trees that was parallel to Arterbury road running up to the start of my school's playing fields and close to the hazy West Wimbledon border between middle class Wimbledon proper and the terraced houses of Raynes Park.

When we worked together building the wall, or in the garden, I heard some of my father's Polish army proverbs.

White Eagle Over Wimbledon

"Everyone is brave until they are shot in the ear." That one stuck in my memory. During my boyhood in leafy Wimbledon there were a few phrases I recall Dad saying that settled in my mind instantly. I knew instinctively that an English father would not use them.

Ireneusz Filipowicz, the author's father, in Polish cadet uniform.

They catalysed a realisation, at first vaguely unwelcome, but then a source of pride, that our family was different from those of other boys at The Squirrels, an unpretentious prep. school near the expanse of lakes and meadows stretching across Wimbledon Common in Surrey to near the Thames at Putney and Richmond, and to my classmates at lofty King's College School, which nestled in a patchwork of green and yellow playing fields across the Ridgeway, where I became a pupil when I was 10.

My father and I had a different background and quirky psychological make-up also, I discovered, to most of the people who lived in the cheerfully prosperous Wimbledon streets where he and Mum made our home.

"People searching a house never look high up," Dad said once reflectively, stashing the quart of Polish vodka in its high fitted cupboard in the corner of the breakfast room.

The remark, startling because mentioned à propos of nothing in particular, recalled his former, clandestine life as Ireneusz Filipowicz, a young man who was often on the run.

With his weapons and explosives hidden in safe houses and a cyanide pill in his jacket lapel as proof against torture, he was in this previous incarnation a fighter in the AK, the *Armia Krajowa* or Polish Home Army, hunted first by the Nazi Gestapo and then by the NKVD, the Russian secret police.

Dad rarely talked about what he did in Lublin, the historic city near the Russian border where he was a student and took the Resistance codename Gryf, (meaning griffin, a fabled creature that is half eagle, half lion) when he was 18 before he finished his studies at his lycée and Poland's underground high school.

Our mother would give my sister Diana and I accounts – blowing up trains and Germans, apparently. We gleaned

White Eagle Over Wimbledon

some insights from occasional flashback remarks he made, hints that 20 years on he was still coming to terms with vivid experiences from Poland's war.

Later, after Dad died suddenly at what seemed to us the very early age of 60, breaking all our hearts, I wanted to try and record some snapshots of the world of Polish former soldiers' lives in Britain.

I fully appreciate that my memoir is subjective. Most Wimbledonians are not much interested in Polish matters while few Poles care what people think of them in London.

My first breakthrough in the quest came when the Polish Underground Trust in London sent me a large brown envelope containing a military curriculum Dad had written by hand in Polish in 1946.

"Sabotage Squad" and "Intelligence" were words I could understand amid references to long disbanded units such as Platoon B, District 5, Lublin.

I puzzled to decipher a military odyssey that took Dad through service in three armies before he settled in England.

"A small group of determined people can cause a lot of damage," was the most I could elicit from him usually if we discussed his time as an Underground soldier.

Or else: "I survived the war not because I was braver than anyone else, just because I was luckier."

It was enough to seem glamorous to a boy, bonding me with friends whose fathers also had been in the Army.

I swapped stories with Andrew Melnick, a classmate whose Polish father took part in the British Army withdrawal from Dunkirk. "He just kept throwing away equipment weighing him down as they retreated to the beaches," Andy said, "By the end they had thrown away nearly everything."

Yearning for romantic adventure, I fantasised that my father was training me for some underground struggle, or wanted to, just as his own father would have done with him in Poland, indoctrinating Dad in what was called "good conspiratorial practice."

This was, on the face of it at least, absurd. Despite the Cold War there seemed little prospect to us schoolboys of Wimbledon being attacked by hostile powers in the carefree 1960s and 1970s, other than by the annual influx of fans at the All England Tennis Club for the centre court championship.

The rest of the year our sprawling mansion-style, seven-bedroom house just off Wimbledon Hill, 10 minutes' walk from the Common, was an idyllic place.

One historian asserts that "guide books do not exaggerate when they claim that Wimbledon is the most beautiful, dignified and refreshing of all suburbs which adjoin the greatest capital in the world …" [10]

"In it men and women may live near the enjoyment of almost complete rural scenery and yet be within eight miles of Leicester Square."

White Eagle Over Wimbledon

In the 1970s on Sunday mornings the actor Oliver Reed[11] could be seen, unshaven and in shorts, buying provisions at the General Stores' vast delicatessen in the High Street as he nursed a hangover. The Pony Club met on Saturday mornings.

My sister Diana recalls that life in 'Wimbles' was magically full of socially mobile, endearing eccentrics, of whom Dad was seen by friends as a colourful example.

Some Wimbledonians were nouveaux riches, like Lew Grade, the impresario, whose Jewish family fled Russian pogroms.

There also were locals with "old money" such as Sacha Baverstock, Diana's friend whose mother had been Deb of the Year, or Laurens Van der Post, the writer who was godfather to Prince William.

Mum and Diana were occasionally invited to tea by Mrs Aitken, a Sloane Ranger type who lived next door to us in a house full of beautiful antiques she shared with two highly-strung Siamese cats.

"She was like something out of Country Life, circa 1930," Diana recalled.

The mass of 99 percent white English people lived in neat detached homes with manicured gardens in what was then the home county of Surrey with its rural villages and stock broker belt towns.

Thousands of men would, like my father, take the fast train each day for a 13 minute journey clattering past

Clapham Junction to Waterloo, followed by a brisk walk across the Thames to the City.

Not everyone in Wimbledon settled into such predictable routines. One night I was woken in the early hours by rousing singing from the road in front of my bedroom window.

Looking out, I recognised beyond our front garden on the other side of the street the handsome features of Patrick Bishop, the elder brother of a friend from Wimbledon College, the Catholic establishment that rivalled King's. He was reeling steadily down the street with an arm over the shoulder of a fellow reveller as they sang, evidently retiring after a convivial evening.

The young men's singing died away as they reeled towards south Wimbledon, passing the home down the street of King's headmaster Frank Shaw who may have glanced out to see if he recognised them as pupils, and heightening my desire to live life to the full.

One of Patrick's sisters married Marek Polanski, a Wimbledon Pole who died aged 31 in 1979. Patrick dedicated a novel to him in which a wartime Polish pilot and an Irish soldier compete for a woman's love.

After becoming a well-known war correspondent and author Patrick spoke fondly of his street in a quiet part of Wimbledon where he grew up.

White Eagle Over Wimbledon

"I have an enduring love for both places and feel a deep attachment to the nondescript streets of places like Morden, Berrylands and the less posh parts of Wimbledon" he said.[12]

Our Wimbledon home after a rare snowfall. Photo: Diana Phillips

Each day I walked to school in the furrowed black sand horse tracks under the spreading chestnut trees of the Common, or cycled along the Ridgeway past a sweet shop filled with sherbet dabs and the august Wimbledon Village Club, a haven for old gentlemen, where diarist John Evelyn had lived.

Further down the Ridgeway was the slightly unsavoury King of Denmark public house favoured by Sixth formers playing darts and poker with languid young women.

"Stop betting now," one of these mysterious, leggy creatures told me kindly in the King after I had, at age 13, wagered a few shillings on an evening when the pub was lit by candles during a power cut, making it seem more an 18th century den of iniquity than ever.

"They're going to start playing for pounds."

By then Dad could be said to have reproduced in England something reminiscent of the lifestyle previously enjoyed by the Polish gentry. The financial prosperity would not endure but his children enjoyed private education and inherited a legacy of resilient values. The memory of his indomitable spirit and kindness were an inspiration.

Dad worked incredibly hard and rarely took me out alone. We did go to see Thunderball, the James Bond thriller, at the Odeon Cinema on Wimbledon Broadway.

We burst out laughing at the end when the secret agent, played by Sean Connery, and his girl, Dominique "Domino" Derval, played by former Miss France Dominique Auger, were rescued by a sky hook-equipped U.S. Navy aeroplane after outwitting the Spectre scary Russian-backed terrorist outfit.

Family picnics were enjoyed on a blanket spread on Wimbledon Common in the meadows near the restored windmill in which Robert Baden Powell in 1908 wrote Scouting for Boys, the bible of the Scout movement.

There were meals at the Wimbledon Tandoori or on birthdays at the fashionable San Lorenzo Italian restaurant.

White Eagle Over Wimbledon

There were also difficult times. Our Latin master, Johnny Rosser, had warned new boys starting school in the Lower Remove that "Gentlemen, life is tough, rough and desperately unjust." [13]

When I was 11, Dad was stricken by a mysterious illness. He passed months at the Atkinson Morley Hospital for nervous diseases whose vast grounds along Cottenham Park road included a patch of land where my scout troop, the 10th Wimbledon, had its headquarters, (about an hour's march from the Windmill on the Common).

Mum in the Army, circa 1949

According to Mum, the doctors thought he would die, but, fortunately, he didn't. Mum smuggled in a half bottle of whisky he drank to ease the pain. Dad kept it under the mattress and shared it with his neighbour in the ward. He spent more months convalescing at home afterwards, and was sometimes belligerent.

"You move like a fly in shit," he complained, waving a walking stick from his sick bed that had been made in the dining room.

Perhaps that was how he galvanised subordinates when he was "a sergeant with the power of a major," as he told it, in the Polish Communist Army, part of the Red Army into which he had been conscripted unwillingly after the nationalist Home Army was outlawed by the Russians.

On rare occasions he certainly scared the hell out of me, not because any physical punishment might be meted out – there never was any – but for fear of losing his love and respect, which was then the most important thing in my life.

Dad's illness most likely was caused by over work.

Wimbledon was where the Phillips family finally came to rest and prosper after a peripatetic existence.

The family odyssey started in Yorkshire, where I was born. I recall running with my mother to catch a tram in Leeds. Dad and Mum, a Lancashire girl and considerable beauty who worked first in the Army pay Corps and then as a researcher at the Daily Express, met after he started working as a textile engineer.

"When I finished college in 1949, I did look forward to some family life, somewhere," he wrote to me later.

White Eagle Over Wimbledon

"My romance with Mama proceeded very quickly, from meeting in summer of 1949 to marriage in February 1950 ... A foreigner is always very susceptible to kindness of the natives as he has no friends and family of his own to help him in a moment of crisis." [14]

American writer Martha Gellhorn, who befriended Polish officers in Italy, lampooned in a short story the kind of English women with whom she claimed they became entangled.

"The girl was perhaps six feet tall, and enormous. Her body was built on the heroic scale of the Winged Victory and though she would be colossal in Greek draperies at the top of the stairs in the Louvre, you did not expect to meet a Greek statue in Grimsby, wearing ugly patent-leather slippers and a slate-blue crepe dress."

A colonel remarked that the girl would marry Sim, a former lieutenant.

"Why not? She is not Princess or Countess. And she is a good woman, everything is good. She loves Sim: she is not afraid of what life he will have ... you must be a Pole perhaps to understand."

"We come very far away, but that is not strange to us. We always go back but maybe not the same ones who go away. Sim knows. Grace knows this too; she is not a Pole, but she knows, for Sim. For you it is the same life as before. That is good. That is what we all like, but it does not happen so." [15]

Mum, too, although beautiful, unlike poor Grace, was fearless, not afraid of what life she and Dad would have.

Soon big wooden packing cases were being stuffed at our Yorkshire house in Heaton Avenue, Keighley. We moved south to a newly built house at Camberley near Sandhurst.

Dad and I built snowmen there at Christmas in the big garden surrounded by countryside and a tranquil Anglican church. I made friends with Army brats at the local ballet school. Dad took flying lessons at a nearby aeroplane club.

We upped sticks again to Wembley in north London where we lived in Old Church Lane. There one also found Poles, including Gen. Bor-Komorowski, the AK commander. His son Adam attended St. Benedict's school in Ealing. Adam wrote of the general (in a memoir sent to Norman Davies) that "He was truly an officer and a gentleman. But to me he was just a father."

Dad moved to London to join Urwick Orr and Partners, a management consultancy founded by Major Lyndall Fownes Urwick, an influential business consultant.

Urwick Orr became one of the leading companies of its type in the 1940s and 1950s. Urwick saw service in the First World War trenches, and won a Military Cross. Men with a good war record like Dad were precious recruits.

Previously Dad worked at Prince Smith, a Yorkshire textile firm that made bayonets in the Second World War.

White Eagle Over Wimbledon

Only twice were my Polish grandparents allowed to visit from Poland. Neither spoke English.

My grandfather, Waclaw, and I played chess in the peaceful living room looking onto the garden of the big house while my father worked at his job as "Head of Special projects" in Unilever, the multi-national company.

We knew that it was stressful work. He brought home mountains of work frequently, and had to practise the different languages he used on travels to destinations as varied as Japan, Portugal, Spain and Venezuela. No language was insurmountable for him.

Late at night, as I listened to Radio Caroline, I heard Dad asking Mum where she put his sleeping pills.

"Mis, where are the Mogadon?" Mis, a little bear in Polish, was Mum's nickname.

Keeping up his new 'cover' identity as Mark Phillips, rather than Ireneusz Filipowicz, perhaps caused part of the stress.

Mum often staged dramatic fits of jealousy when he spent long spells abroad on business trips.

When she was difficult he would whistle a stoic, Slavic tune. "It's from the music to the film of Dr Zhivago," he told me.

The resonance was obvious for Dad in Pasternak's account of how cataclysmic historic events affect families and human love.

He and other Poles found comic relief in *How to be an Alien*, a bestseller about being a foreigner in Britain, written by George Mikes, a naturalised Hungarian.

"It is shame and bad taste to be an alien, and it is no use pretending otherwise," Mikes wrote in the preface.

"There is no way out of it. A criminal may improve and become a decent member of society. A foreigner cannot improve. Once a foreigner, always a foreigner. There is no way out for him. He may become British; he can never become English." [16]

Dad hated working in Nigeria most because of the corruption and endemic violence.

A Unilever colleague, Bill Haines, was ambushed by machete-wielding bandits who shot his driver as he drove into his expatriate compound in Lagos.

"He thought they were going to cut his prick off." English swear words used rarely but in a non-colloquial way were another bizarre and mildly shocking sign to me that Dad originated from a strange world. English schoolboys in the 1960s used different vocabulary that was not necessarily less earthy but was familiar.

Even a seasoned traveller like Dad found Nigeria depressing. He would return to Wimbledon looking exhausted with stories of Nigerians grilling lizards in the street and compulsively buying bottles of Guinness marketed as "white man's blood."

White Eagle Over Wimbledon

In Nigeria, however, Dad again showed his dedication to helping his relatives no matter where they were. He travelled hundreds of miles to visit Kazek, a cousin from Poland who worked as a doctor in a remote Nigerian clinic in the bush.

I became accustomed to Mum calling me to the phone when Dad was travelling. We would have a rushed 30 second conversation while he was in New York, Australia, Nigeria or Venezuela. "Hurry up, this is a very expensive phone call!" he would often say, somewhat illogically.

One day my mother asked me a difficult question. "Would you like to go to a different school on Saturdays to have Polish lessons?"

I wasn't keen, it sounded like another chore and a difficult one, on top of homework. It would have jeopardised my weekly fixture to play cricket on Wimbledon Common, a high point of the summer.

Each week sitting in my classroom learning Latin declensions with Johnny Rosser I would look out of the window at the Rushmere pond in anticipation of week-end freedom with bat and ball.

Chapter 3:
Brazilian interlude

The family upheavals did not end in London. One moment I was enjoying watching the Manchester City football team play in the cup final at Wembley Stadium with my English Uncle Harry near our first London house.

The next a stewardess was waking my sister and I in the first class cabin of a BOAC Comet airliner serving us bacon and eggs as we flew to Brazil where Dad was to work as a consultant.

At a refuelling stop in Dakar, Senegal, I slipped on the runway and lodged my foot alarmingly in a drainage grill, delaying departure by 20 minutes as airline staff struggled to free me, an incident that in retrospect was perhaps an ominous harbinger of future travails in foreign parts.

In the sprawling grounds of the Escola Britannica, the seedy British School in Sao Paulo, I formed my own gang of eight-year-old toughs, English, Americans and Brazilians, who fought a Brazilian-led rival band.

White Eagle Over Wimbledon

Academic standards were atrocious compared to my prep. School in Wembley. The headmaster, Mr Ross, was a former shoe salesman, one of few Englishmen available in Brazil to fill the post.

Our black cook taught us a smattering of Portuguese, mainly necessary for use at the school tuck shop.

One day her husband, a police officer, arrived outside our house, drunk and brandishing a pistol, screaming that he wanted to kill her. The cook, Mum and I cowered inside, confirming our view that England had been a very peaceful place.

More exhilarating were week-end trips down winding mountain roads by chauffeur-driven car to Santos, a faded Atlantic resort surrounded with dirt poor shanty towns, where we stayed in a seaside hotel infested with cockroaches known as *baratas*, and magical holidays on Jequita Mar, a dazzling island with stunning white beaches.

We also made side trips to fly to Buenos Aires. The Argentinian capital's red British-style post boxes and a branch of Harrods again recalled England. At my Brazilian school boys fought with Argentine gaucho lassoes weighted with rocks and strips of barbed wire.

One day in Sao Paulo a military coup suddenly filled the city with automatic gunfire. The first flickerings of discomfort at the sound of shots fired in anger rippled through my stomach during this baptism of fire at age 8.

Brazil, like Poland, was another Cold War battlefront. Its leftist President, Joao Goulart, had irked the military by decreeing agrarian reform and rent controls in March 1964. A rally against the government in Sao Paulo put 500,000 people on the streets.

The U.S.-backed military revolt against President Goulart started March 31. The army garrison at Rio de Janeiro fought against a few troops loyal to Goulart and soon controlled the city. A general strike failed. Goulart fled to Uruguay.

After constant harassment in the street by young leftist students who thought we were Americans and daubed "Yankee go home" on the walls of our house, Mum grew sick and tired of living in Brazil. Dad, who loved the country, reluctantly agreed to move back to dreary, rainy England.

I would miss the sunshine, the beaches of Jequita Mar and the thrill of watching small boys on bicycles hanging onto the back of the battered school bus that collected me each morning. For Dad it meant renouncing an enjoyable expatriate lifestyle surrounded by Latin culture that recalled his youthful days in the army in southern Italy.

As a consolation prize, we sailed back to Southampton by P and O liner ending our 14 months stay in Brazil. It was a heavenly trip with stops at Montevideo and Lisbon and stunning, balmy weather during the four day Atlantic crossing.

White Eagle Over Wimbledon

Passengers played deck quoits, enjoyed ice-cream eating competitions. The sound of third class passengers playing guitars on the lower decks wafted up to the liner's pool as I learned to swim.

Laughter from the passengers in evening dress rippled toward us one night when Diana and I wandered in our pyjamas and dressing gowns into a magnificent ball on the ship looking for Mum and Dad.

There were six years between Diana and me. I imagined as we walked on the high decks of the liner that I would dive in the ocean and save her should she fall overboard.

The Old Church Lane house and its rockery gardens was rented while we were in South America. Dad sold it after we got back to start a new family chapter south of the Thames.

Another of the relatives who came to stay with us there from Poland was cousin Mirek, a good candidate to be the black sheep of the family.

A British general who lived in Poland for 20 years between the wars, Sir Adrian Carton de Wiart, noted in his memoir that "the Poles are among the most hospitable people in the world, and the big houses are nearly always afflicted with a species of permanent guest, or less politely known as a hanger on."

Gen. Carton de Wiart, was a larger than life figure who lost a hand and an eye in the First world war. He was described often as "more Polish than the Poles."

He continued that "he may be a relation, a friend, or merely an acquaintance, and he comes to stay for a night or week-end and proceeds to settle himself down for the rest of his life." [17]

Uncle Mirek fitted this description during his long sojourn at Belvedere Drive. A somewhat feckless journalist and lothario, he made blasphemous remarks when we attended the Polish Mass at the Church at Wimbledon Park.

"I came all this way to go to a fooking church," he muttered during the solemn service.

Uncle John may have had a drinking problem that made him somewhat unpredictable, but he was infinitely preferable to the disreputable Mirek.

I revered my uncle and other wartime aviators, reading countless "Biggles" novels about adventures of a fictional British flier hero.

"Do you know what you want to do when you grow up?" the master who interviewed me at King's College asked. "I want to be a pilot like my uncle."

King's had solid links to the RAF. One of five Victoria Crosses awarded to former boys from the school since its foundation, had been won by a pilot who waged a solitary battle against the Japanese in Malaya despite overwhelming odds, Squadron Leader Arthur Stewart King Scarf.[18]

Most of the Poles living in London in the 1950s and 1960s were former soldiers and airmen and their families.

White Eagle Over Wimbledon

Less than 20 percent of the Polish military in Britain at the end of the Second World War – about 30,000 people in all – decided to return to Poland.

The RAF helped by taking about 500 airmen into its ranks. Others took posts as commercial and test pilots and as technical experts for aircraft manufacturers.

Many refugees were impoverished. General Bor Komorowski, formerly the owner of a wonderful estate in Poland, survived in near poverty in London mainly thanks to his wife making curtains she sold.

The family of Adam Kosterski, who offered to undertake research for this book, was another example of the unusual fortunes of Poles in Britain.

"I was born in London, first generation post war Pole, to a father who was in his late 50's and to a young woman from Warsaw who journeyed to the UK in the mid 50's, and who was just in her teens and living on the east side of Warsaw in Praga at the time of the uprising," he told me.

"My father also served under Anders, initially in Palestine and later through Italy etc. He was assigned to Generał Rudnicki, and was probably part of his personal bodyguard. Like your father, he never came back to Poland, dying in 1984."

"However, unlike your father, his journey to serve under Anders was via the Soviet work camps in Kołyma from which he was released when Britain and Russia became allies."

"I was brought up in a very conservative Polish home. Initially (11 years) our accommodation was a bedsit in a terrace house for Polish invalids in West London, as my father never thought he would marry and didn't buy a house when he had the chance."

"I am the oldest of three brothers and the only one who felt his calling was to 'return' to Poland."

Gen. Rudnicki also found himself in London as what Adam Zamoyski described "a nobody" after having led the attack on Phantom Ridge at Monte Cassino, the liberation of Bologna, won the DSO at Ancona and taking command of the First Armoured Division during the advance into Germany.

"Like so many others, Rudnicki had to face a life of exile, living in penury as a nobody in London, where he was joined by his wife and two daughters (a third had been killed in the Warsaw Uprising)," Adam Zamoyski wrote.[19]

Rudnicki did a number of jobs, at one stage running a junk-shop, and ended up restoring antiques. "However poor he was, he always managed to look impeccably elegant, even dashing, and good humour was seldom absent from his face."

Zamoyski described him as "a product of the slightly naïve, deeply religious and chivalrous outlook of the minor Polish gentry ... not only a distinguished soldier ... but a man of such probity that he resembled one of those shining

White Eagle Over Wimbledon

icons of Christian knighthood which used to be peddled as examples to the young."

General Rudnicki was a neighbour of ours in Wimbledon Park.

While he was eking out a living restoring antiques and running his junk shop, Dad brought into our lives another Polish general living in reduced circumstances as a dedicated artist in London. He was equally chivalrous.

Dad and me

Chapter 4:
Double patriotism

Colonel Ludwik de Laveaux, a tall, distinguished man with a shock of white hair, lived in a tiny bedsit with his wife in the west London suburb of Ealing eking out a living by painting decorative plates and landscapes. Many Poles settled in Ealing near to what had been the big wartime Polish Air Force base at RAF Northolt on the West Circular Road.

"He played a big part in the defence of Warsaw," my father told me when I met the Colonel for the first time. I had no idea what that meant at the time, but it was evidently important from my father's respectful tone. Like Uncle John, the old man was evidently a shadow of his former self. He also was apparently unable to speak more than a few words of English.

His long, distinguished military career, however, spanned the dramas of Polish 20th century history. A survivor of the rigours of the Nazis' Colditz prison, he once made me live on 'prison rations' of porridge and water for two weeks, an experience he may have thought would toughen me up.

White Eagle Over Wimbledon

I experienced his brand of iron military discipline when the Colonel and his wife moved into our house to look after it, and me, while Mum, Dad and Diana were away on holiday in the Canary Islands.

The house-keeping money that Dad had left the Colonel's wife while I was in their charge was not to be squandered wastefully, or perhaps their lack of English prevented them shopping.

Each evening dinner of boiled porridge was served and then re-heated for breakfast. If it weren't for my school lunches I would have gone totally barmy eating only porridge every day for a fortnight. The Colonel believed it would do me no harm to sample the kind of grim diet he had to survive on as a prisoner of war.

Despite such eccentricity, Colonel De Laveaux was a respected artist as well as a soldier. His stark landscapes painted in Colditz exhibited at the Imperial War Museum, where one of them still can be found.

Such Polish "artists made drawings in POW camps and even concentration camps" Douglas Hall wrote in his study of Polish artists in Britain, "the awful circumstances in which they worked provided the most basic and ultimate test of artistic sincerity and natural ability." [20]

Twenty-four paintings by Col. Delaveaux were incorporated in a history of the Polish Legions but the originals were destroyed during the Warsaw Uprising.

Mrs de Laveaux, an example of a short woman mutually attracted with a very tall man, made costume jewellery at home from kits.

Witold Gombrowicz, the iconoclastic Polish émigré writer beached in Argentina during the war, poked fun gently at such genteel Polish women in exile "who, in emigration, work as seamstresses, maids, salesclerks …" [21]

"To what does this ex-lady aspire in the new circumstances? Not to stop being a lady for even a moment! She wants to dress elegantly, even though that elegance must of necessity be impoverished."

"She wants to be fashionable even though she cannot afford the latest fashions … you can talk to her for hours and it would never occur to you that she has experienced something else, something very ruthless."

The Colonel had found himself in a leading role in the herculean task of defending Warsaw in 1939 as commander of the 1st divisional infantry in the Polish 8th infantry division.

He was deputy commander to Lt. Col. Teodor Furgalski, spearheading the fierce fighting around the Modlin fortress north of Warsaw. Furgalski was a sick man during the campaign. Col. Delavaux had to take over day to day command of the division and the stand at Modlin for much of the battle. Both men were taken prisoner. Furgalski died in November of wounds.

White Eagle Over Wimbledon

Promoted to brigadier general in 1964 by the Polish Government in Exile, to us he was always Colonel De Laveaux.

Gen. De Laveaux's decorations included the Virtuti Militari, Poland's highest military award for bravery. Modlin's last stand for Poland was recorded in Churchill's history of the War.

As a young man DeLaveaux had served in General Pilsudski's Legions, and was on the Supreme Command of the Defence of Lwow against the Ukrainian Army in November 1918.

During Poland's war against Russia, the "Miracle on the Vistula" in which Poland saved the West from the Bolsheviks, Delavaux was chief of staff of the 5th Infantry Division.

His son, Ludwik or "Bob," one of my father's Underground comrades, fought in the Warsaw Uprising together with his sister, Hanna. Bob studied with Dad in Scotland and Yorkshire.

Bob was christened Ludwik like his father but used his Underground alias Bob as his first name after emigrating to Los Angeles. He was a member of Lawy Company in the Kampinos Home Army group led by Tadeusz Gaworski.

Kampinos Forest, now the Kampinos National Park, is close to Warsaw, stretching 25 miles to the west and at its widest point 12 miles north to south.

There are large expanses of forest and marshes where AK groups were based and reception committees for air drops organised. Hanna's underground aliases were "Dot" and "Kropke."

Bob de Laveaux slotted into the dynamic, affluent echelons of the American Polish diaspora or Polonia, but died in a horse-riding accident. Feb. 1, 1961. His commanding officer, Gaworski, also died young tragically in a freak accident in 1963.

The British Security Service file on Dad included a letter by the secretary of the Committee for the Education of Poles in Great Britain to the Home Office Aliens Department referring to I.Filipowicz, L.De Laveaux and R.Wesolowski.

"The above named students have been granted permission to transfer from Dundee Technical College to Huddersfield Technical College where they intend to pursue their studies in textiles."

All I knew of Bob was a snapshot in our family photo album showing Bob and his wife Ida standing proudly in front of a gleaming Cadillac he acquired in America. His sister Hanna died in England in 1978. Later I found a family history left by Hanna in the archives of the Imperial War Museum.

"When war broke out my brother was 12 and I was 16," Hanna wrote in a note she left with the file, which I

White Eagle Over Wimbledon

suspected I was the first to read many years later. "It was not too young to join an underground organisation at 12. Communiquès, orders, underground press etc., were usually distributed by children."

"Later he joined the guerrilla operations in the country, chiefly forests, but before, as a very young teenager, (he) disarmed with empty hands a German soldier waiting at the bus stop after curfew hour to get his first weapon."

"At the time of (the) Warsaw Rising he was stationed at the Okecie airport. They were cut off but broke through and joined units in the Kampinos forest. Snap attached. The snap is original taken during one of the battles."

The photo shows a very handsome, tough looking young man with a corporal's flashes on his shoulder and a row of medal ribbons.

Hannah added that "it was in late spring 1945 when they were told to bury the arms and ammunition and disband. Bob (as he was always called at home) set (out) on foot from Cracow over the mountains to Prague. He walked the whole distance. In Czechoslovakia he used his real French name to pose as a Belgian expatriate and via Belgium he reached England and joined the Polish army here."

"But my brother died young."

Hannah also cast some new light on her father's story. "When my father was in Colditz he was on the escape commando. He had to have a hernia operation and they sent him to Colditz hospital. All his clothes were taken away but he was guarded day and night."

After convalescing in Italy at the end of the war the Colonel made his way to England in poor health from his long emprisonment. "He was in Iscoed Park Hospital near Whitchurch in Shropshire for a few years with tuberculosis and recovered," she wrote.

When Princess Elizabeth visited the hospital the colonel and six other disabled Polish ex servicemen gave a Polish gift to the future Queen, a teaset painted by him.

"But he never recovered from the death of his son," Hannah said.

Ryszard Wesolowski, a lifelong friend of my father who in England took the name Merriman, like Bob fought in the Warsaw Uprising – another person, evidently, who was "not an easy man to kill."

He was a soldier in the élite "Baszta" (Bastion) regiment's "Karpaty" battalion, K-1 company that took part in heavy fighting in the Mokotow district.

When Dad told me that "we are all brave until we are shot in the ear," he added; "as Richard Merriman used to say."

Richard's nom de guerre was 'Sten.' In England after the war after studying with Dad and Bob in Dundee and Huddersfield, Richard Merriman became a successful businessman and bought a house in south Kensington.

White Eagle Over Wimbledon

When Dad became badly ill with his mysterious illness a visit by Richard helped to restore him to health.

Mr Merriman died in Paris in May 2011 aged 85. His aristocratic Polish wife Barbara died two years later. She and her daughter, 'Pusi,' were close family friends visiting us often in Belvedere Drive.

Discovering in 2016 that Richard Merriman had been alive until after I started writing this memoir was a hard blow for me that left me depressed for several days. Had I known that he was alive and succeeded in contacting him, he would surely have had much to tell me. Such are the fortunes of war!

Mr Merriman in 2004, however, did give a long, insightful oral history interview about his adventures as an 18-year-old corporal in the Uprising to the online memorial to all participants that is run by the Uprising Museum.

His elder brother was killed on the first day of the insurrection. He was in the thick of much fighting, praising the 'marvellous' quality of his officers such as 'Major Foreman,' Joseph Hoffman. The nearby Red Army's perfidious failure to intervene to help the AK decided Richard not to return to Poland after the war.

While critical of the AK command's bad tactical decision to try and capture the Warsaw Airport with virtually no weapons against German tanks and armoured cars, a suicidal episode of the Uprising that cost many lives, Richard concurred with most survivors that the decision to launch the insurrection had been justified and said the worst moment was when his unit was ordered to surrender.

While Richard and Bob were fighting in Warsaw and Dad in Lublin, Bob's father was languishing in Colditz. A British prisoner who successfully made a "home run" from Colditz, P.R. Reid, recalled that "the Polish contingent ... numbered 80 strong and had been at Colditz from the beginning of the war."

"They were already there when I arrived from *Sonderlanger* of the First World War, Spitzberg and Hohenstein, from where they had registered twelve gone-aways and three home runs to the Polish Underground. Tragic, indeed to recollect that they had no homeland that they could make for."

"When they succeeded in breaking out of the Castle they headed for Switzerland, Sweden or France, leaving their homes and loved ones farther than ever behind them." [22]

Half a dozen Poles escaped from Colditz (gone-aways) but though some of those reached the Swiss frontier they were caught.

After the Poles were moved from Colditz in 1942 at least two, Feliz Jablonowski and Tony Karpf, escaped from a camp further east in Germany and made their way to France and England.

In Italy and England, the Colonel spent three years in hospitals recovering some of his health that had been all but broken in captivity.

White Eagle Over Wimbledon

He was a relative of Stanislaw Ludwik de Laveaux, an aristocrat of French origin, an internationally celebrated late 19th century painter mentioned in much Polish literature. Ludwik was from a French family that settled on Poland in the 18th century.

In 1889 Ludwik also moved to France where he died of tuberculosis at age 26 in 1894. In 1890 and 1893 he had anticipated the travels of the Colonel, visiting London and Oxford where he painted portraits and landscapes.

Many Poles who arrived in Britain as young men, like my father, frequently made fortunes in business.

But making ends meet was a real problem for many older refugees unable to adapt. For years a group of senior Polish officers survived by polishing silver at the Ritz Hotel.

Slavomir Rawicz, a dashing Polish cavalry officer, made his name in 1956 with *The Long Walk*, a thrilling account of his escape with a group of other inmates from a Siberian labour camp, and their trek to freedom across the Himalayas and Gobi Desert.

In Britain, by contrast, he ran a guest house with his English wife at Donington purchased with the proceeds of his book. He subsequently worked for a while as window display designer at Hopewells' furnishers in Nottingham. While his book was a best seller serious doubts subsequently were raised on its authenticity that have never completely been explained.

Back at school, I puzzled again over how my background and roots were different from my classmates, but at the same time almost nobody knew.

My father had Anglicised his name before I was born, taking the advice of his boss at the textile firm in the north of England where he worked as a textile engineer. "Eh, Filipowicz, nobody here'll ever know how to pronounce your name."

One day I met the daughter of another exiled Pole who poured scorn our name change, but her father had settled in France, where a large Polish coal mining community (with its own resistance movement) existed before the war.

Poles in France were not subject to the same hostile prejudice that developed in much of English society from the late 1940s onwards with the advent of a Labour Government. She considered herself "completely French," however.

In Krakow, years later, my wise cousin Andrzej noted when I met him that "your father told us he had to change his name to get a good job with a good salary."

Joseph Conrad was the quintessential example of a Pole anglicising his name after becoming a naturalised Englishman, also to escape the Russians, to make himself recognisable in England and avoid what his biographer called "havoc": "No significance should be attached to Conrad's decision to drop his surname, although Poles were apparently prepared to include even this in their charge of apostasy ... Conrad had enough experience of the havoc wrought with his surname during his time at sea – witness his various certificates of discharge – to appreciate the advantage of using a name that the British could pronounce; and he must have realized the needless disability that he would have suffered if he had written novels in English under the name of Korzeniowski." [23]

Nevertheless Conrad went so far as to apologise to Polish friends that he had not taught his English sons Polish.

Some ways Poles avoided "needless disability" were eccentric. Miroslaw Pszkit was the father of actress Daniela Denby-Ashe. Her parents used a telephone directory to find an English-sounding surname. People couldn't pronounce Pszkit.

One found "Denby", the other "Ashe" and they decided to double-barrel the two surnames.

Andrzej arrived in London in 1974, the last of our Polish relatives to visit us who I met. "It was my first trip abroad alone," he recalled, "and the first time I travelled by plane, and also the first time I went behind the Iron Curtain."

"London for me was wonderful, colourful and friendly. I remember the first time I found myself in Wimbledon in front of the entrance gate to your home, on which hung a sign saying: 'beware of dogs.' I thought that since the gate is open there dogs do not have to be very serious, or does not have them there."

"I decided to enter. There were no dogs. Your Dad opened the door. There was welcome and my joy was great."

I was already "under cover" as soon as I went to school.

In reaction I often preferred to think of myself as English as anyone else, an attitude Mum would encourage later. My father saw his future in England rather than Poland.

Communism seemed so well entrenched in Eastern Europe that the possibility of the pro-Russian regime being overthrown in Warsaw seemed a distant dream in the 1960s.

The fate of Czechoslovakia in 1968 when Soviet tanks crunched into Prague, reinforced the bitterness left by the failure of the 1956 Hungarian uprising and of the strikes in Poland that year.

However the young Polish priest from Wimbledon Park church who came to our house told my mother that I must not lose touch with my Polish roots.

If I did not understand and appreciate my Polish background I would feel bewildered and lost as I grew up. His wise words affected me at the time profoundly and turned out to be true.

History later provided answers to the apparent dilemma of conflicting loyalties. Some of the secret agents who parachuted into Poland had exhibited a special kind of double patriotism.

White Eagle Over Wimbledon

The SOE historian M.R.D. Foot wrote that "on the allied side, patriotism held a very large number of SOE's agents – as well as other soldiers, sailors and airmen – steady in their efforts of war."

"Often theirs was a double patriotism, according to the chances of their own birth: Anglo-French, Anglo-Polish, Anglo-Belgian, Anglo-Norwegian and so on."

"They felt love enough for their own countries and their settled ways to be quite sure they did not want those ways upset by Nazis or fascists or any of their friends or followers." [24]

In history class we were taught to distinguish patriotism from destructive nationalism. One of the best-kept secrets of the school was that "Lord Haw Haw," William Joyce, the traitor who broadcast for the Nazis from Berlin and was hanged, attended King's briefly on a foreign exchange.

This was an evident taboo subject, like the Biggs episode, compared to the role of glorious VC winners and other fallen listed on a memorial plaque in the Great Hall.

A couple of years in the RAF section of the school's Combined Cadet Force and some terrifying pilot's lessons enduring wild aerobatics at age 13 in a tiny Chipmunk trainer aircraft shattered my dreams of emulating Biggles and the long lost glory of Uncle John.

One minute I was taking control in the back seat of the aeroplane, clutching the stick as the obviously bored RAF instructor moved the pedals. The next we were plunging toward the ground in a petrifying nose dive.

The aircraft pulled out of the dive at what seemed like last minute before we must surely crash.

"Just some gentle aerobatics," the instructor muttered as we looped the loop and then went into a stomach-churning barrel roll. Back on the ground I staggered dizzily onto the runway and puked.

That memorable first flight was like being in the "dive bomber," the capsule in a big wheel revolving madly at the funfair that arrived at Wimbledon Common each summer, but without the reassuring knowledge that after two minutes the hair-raising experience would be over.

Joe Baggaley, the master who coached the rugby first XV and ran the RAF section, was a hard taskmaster and probably not the most gifted mind in the history department.

Political fifth formers dubbed him a "fascist" after he deliberately slammed his history class door on the head of an insubordinate boy as he threw him out of his classroom.

I passed my exams in meteorology and air navigation, qualifying for a lance corporal's stripe but instead left the glorious Corps for the esoteric Birdwatching Section.

This was a fatuous activity. One could spend an afternoon reading and smoking in Cannizzaro Park, a Georgian stately home with a botanical garden where boys climbed in at night to take LSD.

White Eagle Over Wimbledon

Time spent in the drab peacetime bases of the RAF on trips organised by the Corps convinced me to trawl around for another dream.

A "quiet and sensitive" boy attracted by birdwatching was just the sort of person who would benefit from more contact with the RAF to make him more outgoing and self-reliant, Mr Baggaley argued in a letter to my father. Dad agreed.

But I was unmoveable. We teenage smokers knew that the RAF was for the birds.

I was still fascinated with flying and my uncle's flying past, however. This grew more tantalising when I visited Poland many years later and was told by cousin Andrzej, that Uncle John had flown out of Warsaw the last military aircraft to leave the capital after the Nazi invasion of the country.

Zamoyski recalled the event in his history of the Polish Air Force.

"On Sept. 25, 1939, no fewer than 420 German bombers preyed on the capital unopposed, and it was clear that the city could not hold out much longer. That evening a Polish plane landed in Warsaw bringing orders to the garrison from the high command in Rumania. It flew out again under the cover of darkness, bound for neutral Latvia." [25]

"The following night, 26 September, a number of senior airmen collected together the nine remaining air-worthy planes, and made a dash for Hungary."

Chapter 5:
Rough, tough and desperately unjust

The Pizza Express restaurant in Wimbledon High Street was a favoured hang-out for King's boys and the pretty Irish and Polish girls from the Ursuline Convent School. Italian food then was a novelty.

Returning home from there later than I had promised one cold autumn evening I ran into Dad further down the High street, looking conspiratorial with his dark gray city overcoat collar turned up.

He broke into a smile. "I thought you might have run into some trouble." He pulled a serrated kitchen knife from his pocket to show me he had come prepared for all eventualities. It was not the only time he advised me to carry a knife.

Pizza Express was cool but not rough, unlike some pubs on the fringes of the KCS teenage circuit. Nevertheless Dad was right to be wary.

White Eagle Over Wimbledon

A nearby florist's shop was rumoured to be the base for two brothers who were violent drug dealers supplying kids selling dope at the school.

A year or two before, while walking home in my red King's jacket in the tree-lined stretch of Wimbledon Hill between the stone horse trough at the end of the High street and our road, a man in a Ford estate pulled up next to the kerb and shouted to me from the wheel.

I thought he was asking for directions but as I drew closer saw he was playing with himself as he urged me to get in the car.

I ran off in a state of shock. The predator sped away laughing.

"Make sure you have a knife in your pocket on your way home," Dad advised later. "I prefer you lose your virginity another way."

The vast expanse of heath studded with gorse and woodland that made up Wimbledon Common, where I went running cross country for school twice each week around the Kingsmere and Rushmere ponds, attracted many different kinds of Londoners, not all of them salubrious, as did the funfair that set up at the Common each year.

The Wimbledon News reported on the gay fraternity who met on the Common. They reputedly wore white polo neck jumpers to recognise each other, or galoshes and dirty raincoats with nothing underneath.

They were harassed by boys from nearby council estates who indulged in "queer bashing."

This hit the headlines in August 1969. A young police constable called Davies went for a walk across Wimbledon Common with two local "rangers" – wardens of the park – and their wives.

When they got to Queensmere Lake, "recognized," Counsel said later, "as an international haunt for homosexuals," P.C. Davies was stabbed fatally by a man afterwards committed to Broadmoor.

Thirty five days later a 28-year-old solicitors' clerk, Michael de Gruchy, was beaten to death with boots and sticks on the edge of the Common by a group of young men who had been on a jaunt from their homes at the nearby Alton Estate, looking "for the action."

Also that year Mrs McKay, wife of the Deputy Chairman of the *News of the World*, was kidnapped from her home in sedate Arthur road. Demands for ransom payments were made, a note from Mrs McKay delivered but she was never found. Two brothers named Hosein received prison terms.

Recalling his Wimbledon school days and time at King's in "Goodbye to All That," Robert Graves wrote that "in English preparatory and public schools romance is necessarily homosexual."

"The opposite sex is despised and treated as something obscene. Many boys never recover from this perversion."

White Eagle Over Wimbledon

The atmosphere had evidently changed at King's. The only hint of 'perversion' I encountered among the English staff was after I slipped on the stone steps of the school during a snow storm, fracturing my head badly and losing consciousness.

Waking up in the school secretary's office, I was entrusted to the elderly Army sergeant major, Mr Hedditch, who ran the school armoury for cadets.

The journey to receive 21 stitches at hospital in his car, a Mini, in some considerable discomfort, would have been easier if the doughty sergeant spent less time squeezing my inner thigh.

Hedditch later taught me shooting and was commissioned, ending his days as a Captain. He was CCF staff instructor, a member of the Queen's Bodyguard from 1960 and received an MBE.

"You've been in the wars, how's your bonce?" Frank Miles asked me when I returned.

Whatever happened on the Common at night was of no concern compared to the pleasure one got as a boy from exploring and the sheer sporting thrill of pounding across its muddy paths and meadows.

In spite of our nicknaming it "Queersmere," I loved Queensmere pond from when our Squirrels sports master took us there to swim. In the 19th century it was a favourite place for fighting duels.

Graves complained in Goodbye to All That that Wimbledon was "neither town nor country," but in modern times its semi-rural nature is part of its charm, an enchanting place in which to grow up.

Another First World War poet, Wilfred Owen, often spent holidays at Wimbledon as a boy, coming down from the north of England to stay with a rich uncle and playing on the Common with his brothers.

Running from the Cross Country start line between two oak trees at the Fox and Grapes pub, once a staging post for coaches to London, there was tremendous satisfaction in splashing through the course on rainy days, leading the pack and hawking into the wind to discourage anyone from trying to overtake me.

Some of our neighbours also were different from the mass of English Wimbledonians. The prosperous Irish engineer and his family who lived in the big house at the top of sloping Conway road, the Coolings and their well-behaved son Brefni, for instance, also were formally outsiders.

But being at least half Polish, was disturbingly more different, though I came to regard many of the hard-fighting, hard-drinking and hard-loving Irish as blood brothers.

As a child Mum had been told by her parents "not to play with the Irish." Many of the sons of the Wimbledon

White Eagle Over Wimbledon

Irish community attended Wimbledon College, run by Jesuit priests.

Irish men and women, though, could be said to have been a known quantity in England. Few ordinary English people knew much about the Poles.

The strapping Pakistani guy who sat next to me in our Squirrels classroom, Anil Puri, an accountant's son, was even more different, of course.

He was a bully, making my life a misery for months until I had an odd fight with him that was far from the classic fist fight between the bully and the underdog in Tom Brown's Schooldays.

Instead I found myself kicking my tormentor in the face repeatedly as he laughed hysterically and made no attempt to resist. His existence was no comfort in my search for identity and acceptance.

On the Surrey and South London streets I explored on my racing bicycle with drop handlebars, however, I learned that class counted as much as ethnic origin.

Shouting "you flash cunt," a group of working class boys thumped me in a park after we played football in the Sunday School team.

It had been dim to ask one of them how many gears he had on his bicycle. "How many have you got?" he shot back. "Five." He was kicking me for being superior as I got on the saddle of my bike to try and escape.

John Phillips

Returning home from the game I heard a commotion in the guest room at the back of the house. Looking around the door I saw Mirek's hairy chest and a familiar, married Wimbledon lady sitting up in the big double bed with the sheets pulled up to their necks.

Mirek caught my eye with a furtive glance then stared in front of him saying nothing. Feeling suddenly very depressed, angry and upset, I closed the door.

Like the sergeant major, Mirek did not play by the rules as taught at Christ Church, the Anglican Church on the Ridgeway where my 10th Wimbledon Scout Troop presented colours at the altar.

Mr Rosser's warning that life is "rough, tough and desperately unjust," had proven true again.

The guest room at the end of the corridor was special, also, in that it looked onto the gorgeous cupressus trees that Dad had planted.

During re-organisations of the house this room jutting into the garden had also been a dining room.

It was there that we had lunch one day with my Uncle Harry on a rare visit from 'up North' and the young Polish priest who underlined the need for us to learn about our Polish roots.

In different uses the room was a setting for different visions of aspects of our chequered family history in inspiring, bewildering and bizarre chapters.

Chapter 6:
I am listening

*"From Stettin in the Baltic to Trieste in the Adriatic an
'Iron Curtain' has descended across the continent,"*
Winston Churchill

In 1952 the Chief Constable of Bradford sent a confidential dossier on Dad to the Home Office including "reports regarding the Alien from the Chief Constable of Dundee, the Chief Constable, Huddersfield, the Chief Constable, Oldham, and the Chief Constable of Manchester."

Yorkshire Detective Constable Byrne, explored my father's life in minute detail after interviewing him. I found his report in the long file held on Dad by MI5 for 40 years that I obtained from the National Archives at Kew after lengthy negotiation with the Security Service.

Decades after Dad recounted his escape from the Russians, the account in the stilted language of the

Yorkshire detectives and Chief constables filled some gaps while raising tantalising new clues.

'Gryf' in Warsaw as a conscript of the Polish 'people's army.'

"He is of good character and has a good knowledge of the English language ... about January, 1944, he had joined the Polish Underground Army in Lublin and completed an officers' training course" Byrne wrote.

"In July, 1944, the Russian Forces occupied Lublin and district. The applicant himself favoured the Polish Government in London at the time, as against the Government set up with the backing of the Russian Authorities."

White Eagle Over Wimbledon

"He continued to serve in the Polish Underground Movement but did not disclose his political views to the Polish authorities in control in Lublin at that time."

"In August/September 1944 he was officially mobilised in the Russian controlled Polish Army and by the influence of a Lieutenant Colonel of the same name as himself and an officer in the Polish regular army he obtained a position on the staff in the Veterinary Equipment Department. He was given the temporary rank of Second Lieutenant."

"In about January 1945 he moved with his unit to Warsaw when the capital was re-captured … he still maintained contact with the Underground movement, favouring the Polish Government in London and for this purpose he states that he used the pseudonym of GRYF …"

Who was the mysterious benefactor in the Communist army, a lieutenant colonel "with the same name as himself?"

"Whilst in Warsaw," the Detective Constable continued, "he learned that the Authorities were becoming suspicious of him and he was sent to Soldin in Pomerania in order to collect captured German stores …"

"He decided that this was an opportunity for him to get away from the Lublin Government Authorities and he travelled from Stettin to Berlin on a Russian military train with a false military pass made out by himself."

Szczecin, Poland (known as Stettin in Germany) is an important sea-port city of approximately ½ million people, located on the Oder River, just across the Polish border from far north-east German.

Stettin was captured by the Red Army on April 26, 1945. It was a highly symbolic and fitting place from which Dad was to become what I believe was the first recorded defector from Eastern Europe to the West in the Cold War.

In 1946 Churchill identified the city as one end of the 'Iron Curtain' in his famous speech of that name at Fulton, Missouri.

"From Stettin in the Baltic to Trieste in the Adriatic an 'Iron Curtain' has descended across the continent," Churchill said.

"Behind that line lie all the capitals of the ancient states of Central and Eastern Europe."

It is 154 km (94 miles) from Berlin and the journey in a Russian military train likely packed with tough Soviet soldiers, under the eyes of the NKVD, must have taken at least three or four tense hours.

The whole time Dad would have waited anxiously to see whether a Russian military railway controller might have spotted his travel pass was false, which would have led to his immediate arrest as a deserter and an eventual prison or death sentence.

Adam Broner, who served with the Polish communist army in Warsaw, a contemporary of Dad's, considered deserting but comrades advised him not to try because it was too dangerous.

White Eagle Over Wimbledon

"Several times I had witnessed the punishment of Polish Army deserters by execution." [26]

From Warsaw to Soldin in Pomerania, now the city of Mysliborz in Western Poland, is 500 km, a long train journey in the chaotic conditions after fighting had ended four months earlier.

In all Dad's dash to freedom was over 500 miles (650 km), and may have taken at least two or three fear-packed days with him nervously aware of the cyanide pill in his lapel.

Did he "decide that this was an opportunity to get away" on his own or had he consulted with his friends from the AK in Warsaw before going on the run?

Dad's break for liberty blazed a trail that would be followed by many other defectors, however. He told me that he was "one of the first defectors" but I found plenty of evidence that he was in fact the first of the Cold War from Poland and indeed eastern Europe.

The best-known Polish defector in the early post-war period was Franciseck Jarecki, a Polish Air Force pilot who in early 1953 made a daring escape to the West flying a Mig-15 trainer aircraft from Slupsk to Ronne airport on the Danish island of Bornholm.

In 1949, Lt. Arkadiusz Korobczynski from Navy Flight in Wicko Morskie defected with an Ilyushin M3 attack aircraft to Gotland Island in Sweden.

The Communist attitude to defectors was shown in 1952 when Edward Pytko, an instructor at Dęblin, where Uncle John trained, tried to escape to Western Germany, but was stopped by Soviet aircraft and handed back to the Poles.

Pytko was charged with high treason and executed. The first recorded Russian defector of the Cold War (after World War 2 ended with the Japanese surrender Sept. 2, 1945) was Igor Gouzenko in Canada Sept. 5, 1945.

Dad's defection not more than two weeks later was evidently the first from Eastern Europe defined as eastern countries except for Russia and the USSR and the first in Europe.

Many Polish defectors were tried in their absence and sentenced to death. Hundreds of Soviet defectors were tried in absentia including a number of ordinary soldiers who received the death sentence though having no political or military secrets to pass over.

Airey Neave, who escaped from Colditz disguised as a German officer and went on to work for MI9, in fact noted that escapers often are reluctant to tell their stories.

"People who have worked in resistance movements or prisoners of war do not care to dwell on their experiences. What is thrilling to the reader was frightening to the man he is reading about ... the men, often very young, had been exposed to the feeling of being hunted, sometimes for several months," Neave said.[27]

White Eagle Over Wimbledon

"They hated this cross-questioning and a desire to sublimate their anxiety, added to the rather soulless War Office system, did not allay their fears. The shock of arrival, after weeks of danger and excitement ... increased their reticence."

Dad was in fact very young when he went on the run to the West – just 21 years old.

According to an exhibit organised by the Polish National Institute of Remembrance in 2012 there was, within a year of Dad's dash West, a wave of escapes. Thousands followed in his footsteps.

"According to the estimates of the Polish authorities in London, by spring 1946, each day around 300 people defected via the Pilsen route, where American troops were present at that time."

"This form of opposition against the new, communist reality, was chosen mainly by those who were connected with the independence underground or anti-communist opposition, and whose family members were in the West."

The police report described how Dad was received. Checking his story involved a week in "detention" and being passed from U.S. to British and then free Polish authorities. All subjected him to interrogation to determine that he was not a spy.

"He first contacted the American Authorities in Berlin and then British Military Authorities in Potsdam."

"He was there interviewed by British Military Security Officers and placed in detention for a week for his story as a political refugee to be checked ... Towards the end of September 1945 he went to the 1st Polish Division HQ in Meppen, north Germany where he was again subjected to interrogation by the Polish authorities."

Of this interlude when his credibility was being checked, Dad told me with a smile that during his time in British detention he was set to work peeling potatoes "and was put through all kinds of psychological debriefing."

Later, while I languished briefly in jails in Italy and the Arabian desert, I would take courage from his description of his ordeal as an amusing adventure.

Once Dad was in the hands of the free Polish authorities the worst of his vetting was over.

Messen was part of a Polish enclave centred on the town of Haren set up by Allied authorities from May 1945 to help deal with over 3 million Polish citizens in Germany – slave labourers, concentration camp prisoners or prisoners of war.

It was used as a resettlement camp, local cultural centre and a station from which Displaced persons could be dispatched to Poland or Western states. Many AK members who had been prisoners after the Uprising were moved into Haren.

The enclave town was named Maczkow in honour of General Maczek, the commander of the 1st Armoured

White Eagle Over Wimbledon

Division. It must have been a curious place for Dad to find himself in.

The streets in the town were renamed in Polish honouring various units or after streets in Warsaw. It had a Polish mayor, Polish school and a Polish rectory. The town was returned to its original inhabitants in 1948.

The police report went on to describe Dad's happy period in Italy.

"He was then sent to the 2nd Polish Corps in Italy where he was attached to the 12th Polish Artillery Regiment near Porto San Giorgio [on the Adriatic coast in the Marche region], as a private soldier. During the latter part of November 1945 he was sent to a Polish Officers' Training Unit."

Dad, in Polish 2nd Corps after defecting to the West, with Warsaw Uprising anchor badge on battledress.

"He completed a course of training on 9.7.46 and became a Corporal Officer Cadet. He rejoined the 12th Polish Artillery regiment and then came to England, arriving at Dover Sept. 1, 1946. He was first stationed in Scotland.

"In July 1947 he enlisted in the Polish Resettlement Corps and was relegated to the Reserve, W class, as he began his studies in Dundee and then at Huddersfield."

It is surprising that the police went into so much detail. Evidently this was a requirement of the Security Service, or MI5, which would scrutinise the report.

The police added that "During the time he (Dad) has been resident in Bradford his conduct has not given cause for complaint and he has not been the subject of enquiries from any Government Department. He is not known to be connected with any political or subversive organisation."

Echoing other police reports in the MI5 file he added "he is obviously a man of good education," perhaps not an epithet that carries much weight with the UK police today.

The underground army in the Lublin region, according to historian James Blackwell numbered 60,000 men.[28] The army was created to facilitate the re-establishment of an independent Poland.

As a boy I found Dad's rare wartime recollections he told me puzzling – how he had to lie low when his girlfriend was arrested by the Gestapo, for example, and how his membership of the underground gave him admittance to exclusive aristocratic salons in Lublin.

Once in England, in contrast, he was officially termed an 'Alien,' a term long since dropped.

White Eagle Over Wimbledon

"Alien was attending a secondary school in Lubartow when the Germans invaded Poland continued with his studies until December 1943," Sgt. G. Owen of Manchester Police wrote in 1951.

"In the spring of 1944 he joined the Polish 'underground movement' but when the Russians occupied the area in 1944, all the underground chiefs were arrested and Filipowicz to avoid being arrested joined the Polish Army, although he carried on with his underground activities."

"The Russians discovered this duplicity and Filipowicz obtained false papers and fled to Berlin in 1945 and reported to the military authorities in the Western Zone."

"He was 'screened' and allowed to join the 1st Polish Division H.Q. in Western Germany and was sent to Italy. Where he served until he came to the UK in September, 1946 ..."

"He has no wish to return to Poland because as he says 'I am a deserter from the Polish Army and I dislike Communism.'"

The report on the "Alien" concluded: "Well educated, well mannered, pleasant disposition, very interested in his career, and of no security interest."

Fortunately Dad had not lost patience with the grilling or he might have been forcibly expelled back to occupied Germany, a fate undergone by hundreds of unsuitable Poles.

Neave described how British official reports of soldiers going on the run always seem to underplay the underlying drama. "My adventures were taken down and reduced to War office language. I could hardly recognise them. The account was far less exciting than a report by the C.I.D. on their observation of a public convenience."

The MI5 file on Dad also included a May 1952 War Office record report. "The conduct of the applicant during his military service has been very good," it said – a few notches up the scale from the War Office's judgement on Uncle John's record as just "satisfactory."

Dad's signed Nov. 8, 1952, a declaration that "if naturalised as a citizen of the UK, I will not, when in any country of the Commonwealth, seek the diplomatic or consular protection of Poland, nor claim the benefit of any allegiance that I may still be deemed to owe to Poland under Polish law."

As Mikes said "The verb to naturalise clearly proves what the British think of you. Before you are admitted to British citizenship you are not even considered a natural human being." [29]

Inevitably the surviving official records gave few details of what it was like fighting in the Resistance.

Later I read the story of a young officer in the Lublin underground, Marian T., written by Jozef Garlinski. In summer 1942 many people at Lublin underground headquarters were arrested.

White Eagle Over Wimbledon

Marian was arrested and taken to Akademicka Street, the Gestapo headquarters, and a couple of days later to the tower of Lublin Castle. His ordeal underlined what Dad had risked: "It was all over. His colleagues, arrested at the same time, had broken down and confessed. There were confrontations, they were put in the same cell, they were beaten in front of Marian; he himself was beaten, starved, hung up in chains …"

"He gritted his teeth and said nothing. At last he was thrown into the cell from which there was only one way out, execution." [30]

Marian told Garlinski his story when they were in Auschwitz. "It was just then, when he lay swollen and covered with blood, on the wet concrete waiting for the rattle of keys, that the first miracle happened."

"In a piece of bread he found a scrap of paper on which a woman's hand had written with even letters: 'The others are all dead, but don't be afraid, I am thinking of you. Halinka.' He didn't know anyone called Halinka and couldn't comprehend who it was and how she had managed to smuggle in this mysterious message."

"A week later came a second message. 'I am fighting for you, trust me.' It couldn't be a letter of an informer? Marian experienced a feeling of excitement that he had not felt for a long time … Could it be that he was not quite alone?"

Marian learns that Halinka was the fiancée of an Underground colleague who had been shot. He receives a photograph of her. In the concentration camp he received parcels from her.

Garlinski's chapter on Marian ends as they are separated. "Where are you, what has happened to you?"

AK leader Jan Karski, recalled that "an Underground man, apart for the risk of being caught, with all that capture by the Gestapo entailed, enjoyed considerable advantages over the rest of the population."

"He had the protection of the organisation and its efficient machinery at his disposal. He could secure good personal documents and obtain certificates of fictitious employment.

"He usually received a little money, had a number of addresses to retreat to, homes where he could always find a little food, a bed and a place to hide from Gestapo raids." [31]

"Furthermore he had the peace of mind resulting from the knowledge that he was serving a good cause. He had the dignity of having remained independent and true to his beliefs …"

Karski told another chilling yarn set in Lublin. A school chum, Tadeusz Kilec, was arrested with three others.

"The four had been caught loosening the screws in the railroad tracks. A transport of food and arms was due the next day from Russia to the Third Reich and they were attempting to blow it up." [32]

White Eagle Over Wimbledon

"They were publicly hanged in the market place of Lublin. Their bodies were left on the gallows for two days and nights."

Ruthless Nazi repression of the Lublin Resistance was in part because the city was a major SS and police outpost in eastern Poland "slated for extensive Germanisation," [33]

This was especially the case around Zamość where 100,000 Poles were evicted from their homes in 1942-44. "Though Himmler had grandiose plans to make 40 percent of the people of Lublin German by 1944, he never succeeded."

In July 1944, the situation changed completely when Soviet forces set foot in Lublin province, "aiming to put into place a regime that was compliant and communist," as Blackwell said.

However the decision by regional AK commander Marcin to order his forces to hand in their weapons and disperse meant that "the human stock of the underground would remain, that it would survive the first wave of NKVD arrests."

Because respected officers and their men survived the 1944-45 winter, the Underground remained more organised in Lublin than elsewhere in Poland. It was a sizeable threat to the communist regime in the city until 1947.

Dad spoke fondly of his time in Italy with the Polish 2nd Corps attached to the British Army, where he trained as an artillery officer. He ended the war at Ancona after graduating from officers' training school near Lecce.

Norman Davies captured the spirit of Dad's trip from England to Italy.

"For ex-insurgents who decided to join the 2nd Corps of Gen. Anders in Italy, the prospects were highly exhilarating."

"Having experienced both the horrors of the Rising and the boredom of the prison camps, the journey across the Alps in the spring or early summer of 1945 must have aroused deep feelings of joy and relief."

"As they climbed the Brenner or the St Gotthard Pass in the back of the British army trucks sent to collect them, surrounded by magnificent snow and sunshine, they were leaving their wartime woes behind … they knew that as soldiers of Gen. Bor they were driving to the warmest of welcomes."

Dad looked ecstatic in photos in the mountains of Italy wielding a tommy gun in British khaki battledress, that I leafed through often in our precious family album guarded dutifully by Diana.

When we were in Italy while I was a student once Dad, during a visit he made to me, recalled, as we drove through olive groves in the Tuscan hills, his being reprimanded by one of his gunnery instructors in Italy for hitting the target during an exercise, an olive tree almost out of range.

White Eagle Over Wimbledon

The instructor was maddened at the prospect of having to find a new target. The episode was a bizarre example of the vagaries of army life.

Gen. Roman Odzierzynski, commanding Dad's regiment in 2nd Corps artillery, would be a prime minister of the Polish Government in exile, which kept a lonely vigil for Poland's independence during the 45 years of Soviet rule.

The period of Italian euphoria, of "old wine and young girls," was all too short-lived for Dad and the other 2nd Corps men who Churchill kept stationed at the Adriatic port of Ancona for some 18 months after they liberated nearby Bologna April 21, 1945, at the cost of hundreds of Polish lives.

Artillery training with Polish free forces in Italy.

The Poles remained there, Dad told me, in case they were needed to push back the expansionist Yugoslav

John Phillips

Communist forces under Marshal Tito, still eager to claim Trieste as Yugoslav territory.

Britain denied this after Moscow, on behalf of Yugoslavia, made a protest to the UN Security Council about the Polish 2nd Corps' presence south of Trieste.

After Labour won the 1945 election the Atlee Government was keen to persuade as many Poles as possible to return to Poland while recognising that many could not go back and that for them Churchill's pledge was binding.

Dad on patrol in Italy

During Dad's sojourn in Italy the Polish Armed Forces under British command were disowned by the Communist government in Warsaw Feb. 14, 1946.

White Eagle Over Wimbledon

In March 1946 Dad and the other Polish troops in Italy received a letter from Ernest Bevin, the Labour foreign secretary, urging them to return to Poland.

At the end of September, 1946, a month after Dad landed in Britain, the Polish government revoked the citizenship of Generals Anders, Maczek, Kopanski and dozens of other officers.

Polish elections held in Jan. 1947 were rigged by the Communists, making the prospect of returning to Poland even less attractive to Dad and his comrades in Scotland.

Few could go back to Poland safely. If my father went home he would have been imprisoned and perhaps shot, like thousands of men from the AK.

At first Dad could only telephone Poland and receive calls from Lublin, often spending hours talking to his parents. He sent his first letters to them signing himself as Uncle John.

As Sue Ryder wrote "in those days (the 1950s) it was a triumph to get through to Britain from Warsaw and have the line kept clear." [34]

I understood little Polish but some words I heard Dad saying on the telephone stuck in my memory. All through my teens, for example, I would hear my father say "Suham" when he picked up the telephone.

Years later, taking lessons at the Polish Institute in Rome, I learned its' meaning: "I am listening,"

John Phillips

Perusing my father's file from the Underground Trust I recalled a scene from John le Carrè's thriller, *The Looking Glass War*.

Haldane the spymaster "reopened the file and was looking curiously at the photograph of a Polish boy who had fought the Germans twenty years ago." [35]

"He seems to have a talent for survival," he observed, finally indicating the file. "Not an easy man to kill."

Student days, Dundee. With AK comrade Ryszard Wesolowski (left), Irish and Scots college friends.

White Eagle Over Wimbledon

Dad's 12th Polish Artillery regiment identity card.

Chapter 7:
Roundheads and Cavaliers

Wimbledon remained a pseudo village even when in 1969 it became part of Greater London rather than Surrey. But an intoxicating whiff of the Flower Power era arrived from the London of the Swinging Sixties.

At my first Scout camp in deepest Surrey I shared a tent with my "Wolves" patrol of tough kids from Raynes Park, discovering that boys of 11 drank beer and smoked Woodbines and No 6.

We learned field craft and how to develop night vision from Ian Schluter, our scoutmaster, a robust policeman with a craggy, pock-marked face. He regaled us with accounts of raids he took part in on sado-masochistic brothels in Soho.

During a summer camp on the Isle of Man, Ian disclosed he had a girlfriend. "I always use the same Johnny twice," he said, "of course you have to wash it after the first time."

Scouts from 10th Wimbledon had transistor radios, too. We listened religiously to Radio Caroline and the other

White Eagle Over Wimbledon

pirate radio stations operating from ships anchored off the south coast.

They broadcast songs like "Ha, Ha, said the Clown," Manfred Mann's 1967 iconic hit which seemed to poke fun at middle class London's relentless drive for status and security.

The Kinks' song "Waterloo Sunset," recalling Dad's daily commute to the City battlefield, and the Beatles' "Yesterday," wailed long into many of the nights under canvas.

Crashing through groves of ferns and clumps of nettles on wooded hillsides and lashing together poles into 20-feet high towers that we climbed to scan the surrounding countryside, I found blessed relief from the competitive pressure of school that cranked up as exams approached.

During the long summer holidays, I listened mesmerised at the swimming pool in the King's playing fields to sixth formers who arrived wearing flowered shirts, some accompanied by glamorous girlfriends.

Swimming endless laps as I admired their girlfriends' figures, I heard tell of orgiastic "love-ins" at pop festivals in the Home Counties.

Their new heroes, practising the forbidden cults of free love and psychedelic release, included the stars of *Easy Rider*, the 1969 film, played by Dennis Hopper and Jack Nicholson.

There was a rush to buy motorbikes to speed around Wimbledon Common and its constellation of pubs such as the Crooked Billet and the Hand-in-Hand at night.

One older boy, Jim Payne, seemed to have achieved god-like status, acquiring a Harley Davidson, setting up a rock band and a business producing and repairing stylish Rabbit electric guitars.

James Dacie, the son of a brilliant haematologist at Hammersmith Hospital, Prof. Sir John Dacie, lived around the corner from us in Alan Road. He became a mentor in reading and low life as we cycled to King's or wandered parks scouting for girls.

We loved English and French literature, girls, music, language and the gentle Surrey countryside. James was an accomplished musician, cricketer and fisherman. I smoked my first woodbine with him while we were fishing on the riverbank at Kingston on Thames, casting lines to catch dace and other small fish.

Sir John was a retiring figure who had been a colonel in the Royal Army Medical Corps in the war. At home he relaxed by playing cello with James and building up his butterfly collection.

Perhaps to compensate for shunning Polish lessons, I took a Russian language and history class at school taught by a former Royal Navy officer, Tony Bosworth, who normally taught Latin. I hoped learning Russian would help me to learn Polish without special lessons outside school hours.

For a project, I collected evidence against the Russians for killing thousands of Polish officers at the Katyn forest, a

White Eagle Over Wimbledon

crime Moscow would only acknowledge when Mikhail Gorbachev was president.

"You'll probably end up finding what a lot of historians say," Bozy warned me, "Russian foreign policy under the Communists was a continuation of policy under the Tsars."

This was more than just a school task for me. My grandfather Waclaw had been among the reserve officers rounded up by the invading Russians in Eastern Poland in 1939.

Grandfather managed to slip out of the ranks of doomed officers bound for Katyn and melt away into a crowd of civilians lining the streets of Lublin, living to fight another day. Otherwise he might well have been shot with the others.

It was hard to equate such drama with the gentle man whose blue eyes matched mine as we played chess in our lounge. The war had been hard on my grandmother, Genevieve, also.

"When my mother learned that I had joined the Underground she went to bed for a week," Dad told me.

Jan Karski wrote that "For the mothers, daughters and wives of the men in the Underground, misery was their daily lot." [36]

"If they did not actively participate themselves, then their torment was all the greater because, not having any way of gauging danger or sensing the approach of tragedy, they expected it constantly and never knew a moment's peace."

Grandmother had helped save the family by stockpiling sugar and flour that she sold on the black market. Dad helped by working the night shift in a cheese factory. My grandfather's salary as a civil servant was worth increasingly less. I saw my grandmother for the last time over lunch at the Polish Hearth Club, Ognisko, in South Kensington.

"Janek, Janek," she would say, looking me deep in the eyes and patting me reassuringly on the wrist

A constellation of clubs like Ognisko had sprung up for the Polish community around London.

The Hearth Club with its restaurant serving Polish dumplings and immaculate bar with a vast range of different vodkas, quaffed under portraits of General Anders and President Sikorski, was one of the smartest.

Most exclusive still was the Polish Air Force Officers' Club, sadly since closed, an intelligence dive where for decades patriotic Poles plotted the recovery of the homeland.

Zamoyski, described the club in his study of "the Forgotten Few."

"It is commonly believed that the hall porter worked for the CIA, the barman for British Intelligence and one of the administrators for the KGB and the CIA at the same time." [37]

Sorties to those clubs with Dad in the sophisticated world north of the Thames were special treats as a boy.

Dad showed another side to his character when I threw an impromptu party for my school friends. Scores of long-haired gatecrashers turned up, many high on "acid" and dope.

It was light years from his strict Catholic upbringing in Poland, when Dad served as an altar boy at his local Church. The exiled Polish artist Marian Kraochwil expressed similar reservations when he spoke of "the shallowness and humdrum hedonism of British society." [38]

Scores more guests arrived as the pubs favoured by hippies emptied at closing time.

Marcus Benny, a teenager who dabbled in a myriad of illicit substances, lay sprawled under the drinks table, his pupils dilating fiendishly. I wandered around appalled, powerless to enjoy being host as I waited for the inevitable storm to burst when my parents came down to investigate.

Dad flew into a rage and threw the revellers out physically one by one, kicking some in the pants down the front steps if they were slow to leave. He then raised hell with my headmaster, Frank Shaw, about the drug problem at school. I was called to the headmaster's study.

"Was there a lot of snogging at your party Phillips?" he asked kindly. I was sorry for having unwittingly set off an uproar.

The drama made me a lonely figure of fun. Dad berated me for befriending the dregs of the school.

To compound matters the local barber went to town on me with a skinhead short back and sides that made me even more vulnerable to ribaldry from boys whose fathers had their ears bent by Dad.

Mr Shaw wisely took little notice of parents tilting at windmills over changing times.

As the King's official history wrote "the birth of the permissive age, with all that this implied in pressure on young people's standards of behaviour and academic discipline, threw a particularly heavy burden on the Headmaster of a London day school."

"Without firm guidance, and an implicit indication of what was expected in work and personal demeanour, it would have been all too easy for many boys in the School to have lapsed into the sensuous indulgence urged upon them by the irresponsibility of the mass media."

"Instead it was made clear to them that the dividing line between freedom and licence was not to be crossed."

The tone of Shaw's headmastership set the tone of the school. "Urbane, without a hint of feebleness; liberal, without a suggestion of the woolly mindedness that so often accompanies it: altruistic, yet clear-headed; understanding but never gullible."

The official School history recalls "it was the era of drug-taking among adolescents, when day-boys were open to far greater temptations and opportunities than boarders were. Nevertheless only minimal offences were reported despite the most vigilant surveillance organised among selected Staff members."

White Eagle Over Wimbledon

There was solace to be had, fortunately, breaking through painful shyness in the arms of Eleanor, Lisa, or Jackie, generous girls from the Ursuline High School eager to be "got off with" on the fringes of dances and rock concerts by school bands at Edge Hill Parish hall. Boys cynical perception was that Catholic girls from the Ursuline were more repressed and so more passionate.

Some lucky graduates of the initiation class might progress to enjoy the striking favours of tall, statuesque Irish or Polish beauties with wonderful figures.

Among the stunning girls of Polish origin in our effervescent group of friends was Anna Dubrawska, a serious, very well brought-up young lady. Her family's history was another example of Poles' ability to adapt to exile and prosper.

Anna's father Kazimierz Dubrawski came from a town called Stryj that still baffled Anna slightly when she told me about it years later

"When I looked on the map it now seems to be in the Ukraine which is odd because all his family are from Krakow," she noted, "Very confusing." [39]

Cazimierz was studying economics at university when the war began and he was called up for army service. He was captured early in the campaign and spent nearly four years as a prisoner of war, first of the Germans and then of the Russians "which was far worse."

"I have many stories from this time although as I got older they were more grim," she noted.

He was finally "let out by locals from the area" and fled to Austria helping in displacement of people in 1946. He came to London with his surviving brother. A third brother died in the war.

Kazimierz applied to go to the USA but when his application came through six years later he had met Anna's English mother and decided to stay. His brother was already in Hollywood working as a veterinary surgeon.

In London he was very involved with the Polish community. First he worked part time at the Polish club in Kensington and continued going there and to the other clubs in Hammersmith and Balham.

Mr Dubrawski and his friend M. Magiera started a newspaper for people from his town called Biuletyn Kola Stryjan. It had a large following around the world. It was a point of reference for exiled Polish intellectuals. He sang in the Polish choir at the Church in Wimbledon Park.

Mr Dubrawski became active in politics and secretary of Putney Conservative Party, the power base of the politician David Mellor. The two men became great friends. He wrote letters to Margaret Thatcher on various subjects.

Growing up in England "I never ever heard anything negative about the Poles or my father," Anna said.

White Eagle Over Wimbledon

"At work he was loved for his sense of humour and they always joked about his strong accent but that was only in fun."

Living to the age of 87 he was able to return twice to Krakow after the end of Communism.

As Anna said, "I think he was integral to creating a bit of Poland in the Putney and Wimbledon area."

Although she attended the Polish language school in Wimbledon Park, which I had avoided, Anna claims that she "does not speak Polish at all." This makes me feel less guilty.

She married her teenage sweetheart, Pierre Spake, a popular artist who was at King's with me. Today they live in Hertfordshire.

Anna has never been to Poland but her children have been to Krakow to maintain family ties.

King's arranged dances with Wimbledon High School for Girls where Diana went on Wimbledon Hill Road.

Founded in 1880 as part of the Girl's Public Day School Trust, Wimbledon High through its history emphasized love of learning and encouraged girls to go to university.

Ursuline High School was founded 12 years later. Four nuns from Forest gate came to Wimbledon to establish a tiny school with three pupils in Worple Road.

The school offers a philosophy inspired by St Angela Merici emphasizing poverty and virginity. St Angela founded the Ursuline order in the 14th century inspired by the English St Ursula.

By the 1960s Wimbledon High was a top girls' school. Its brainy emphasis made its bluestocking pupils less attractive to us than sexy Ursuline girls though as a grammar school the Catholic institution was an academically strong alternative.

One or two advanced 14-year-olds in my class at King's like Steve Campbell, bragged about girls who allowed them to put hands up their skirts and explore unimaginable territory. "It's more tiring than running the mile," Steve confided to me with a subversive grin. He boasted of deeds incompatible with the philosophy of St Angela Merici.

Steve was the class expert on such matters, learned from his brother Duncan, who broke many hearts.

"I think you'll be a good kisser, John," Steve said. But the rest of us contented ourselves with groping or reading yearningly popular pseudo medical books like The ABC of Sex. In the pre-internet age there was none of the online temptations facing schoolboys today.

I sought respite from the mockery in the wake of the disastrous party by burying myself in the Metaphysical Poets, T.S. Eliot and Yeats.

The brilliant English literature master, Frank Miles, a disciple of the Cambridge critic F.R. Leavis, taught us to appreciate poetry through close reading and appreciation of writers whose work reflected lived experience.

White Eagle Over Wimbledon

Miles's profound influence was recorded perceptively by the philosopher Roger Scruton.

"At Cambridge I had the good fortune to meet young men who had been educated at KCS Wimbledon, a fee-paying school connected with King's College, London, to which Victorian Bohemians like the Rossettis and (the painter Walter) Sickert had been sent to escape the heartiness of the old public schools ..." [40]

"Its intellectual life was dominated by Frank Miles, a Leavisite master who had instilled the quiet conviction that art matters because life matters and that life is nothing without art ... however much we smile now at the excesses of our teachers they opened the door on the moral and spiritual landscape of England."

Frank wrote the official history of the school published in 1979, spending many hours doing research in the archives of King's College in the Strand.

In the 19th century it was a junior department of King's College at London University and progressive, becoming one of the first public schools to teach science.

Charles Dickens sent his son there but the school's liberal reputation suffered from the death in 1885 of 12-year-old Charles Bourdas, a victim of systematic bullying at the school's premises in the Strand before it moved to Wimbledon.

Bourdas died nine days after repeatedly being punched in the spine by older boys.

Despite offering a pioneering curriculum with an emphasis on drawing and science, the history also lays bare the cavalier treatment of masters when the school struggled to survive financially.

Later Leavis's pioneering concepts propounded by Miles included a liberal idea of Englishness. In his influential work *The Great Tradition,* Leavis ranked Conrad together with George Eliot and Henry James as the greatest English novelists in his concern with form, excluding Hardy and Dickens.

Conrad's Polish background enabled him to develop radical solutions to his fiction's formal problems, Leavis argued. Conrad's concern with moral isolation made him particularly relevant to England of the 1940s struggling almost alone against Nazism.

Robert Graves' book mentioning his time at KCS after it moved to Wimbledon did not suggest there was much escape from heartiness.

"I felt oppressed by the huge hall, the enormous boys, the frightening rowdiness of the corridors, and compulsory Rugby football of which nobody told me the rules," Graves wrote.

He later was bullied at Charterhouse because of his German mother. Raymond Rodakowsky, a half-Polish friend whose father was a founder of Brooklands Racing

White Eagle Over Wimbledon

Track, helped Graves beat the bullies by encouraging him to box.

Dad then found émigré politics stultifying. He preferred to help practically, spending long hours packing up parcels to send to Poland.

The Association of Polish Combatants (SPK) in Britain was formed in 1946. Its manifesto included the continuation of the fight for Poland's freedom, to maintain the traditions of the Polish soldier, to ensure that friendly relations were maintained with the host nation, to bring aid to countrymen.

It sent aid to beleaguered families in the homeland in the form of parcels.

Dad was always returning from sales at Wimbledon shops with respectable jackets or suits he wanted me to wear. Inevitably they were out of fashion. I felt fleetingly guilty as Dad looked disappointed at my refusal. Then he would shrug. "Okay, I'll send it to Poland then."

Politics attracted me. During a spree as the pub closed near King's, I climbed on the roof of a car and made a rousing speech calling for revolution. My parents were Conservative.

Dad generally respected my opinions. He sometimes shared them, even fervently, when we agreed on stuffy aspects of the British establishment agenda.

"I'll vote for anyone who gives northern Ireland back to the Irish," he said. Dad poured scorn on what he called "a good old English compromise."

This was a theme taken up by Mikes in "How to be an Alien." Mikes wrote that "bargaining is a repulsive habit; compromise is one of the highest human virtues – the difference between the two being that the first is practised on the Continent, the latter in Great Britain." [41]

"It is alright to have central heating in an English home, except in the bath room, because that is the only place where you are naked and wet at the same time, and you must give British germs a fair chance …"

A VIth Form friend, James Montgomery, joined the Trotskyite International Socialists. Dad spotted James selling the Socialist Worker newspaper at Wimbledon Station. James soon was declared persona non grata at our house.

"Why do you think I was fighting against the Russians?" Dad asked me as he paced around the breakfast room, a sausage sandwich in one hand and a glass of vodka in the other.

I must have driven him to distraction. I still didn't really understand how he could have fought the Russians as well as the Germans. It made no sense until later though for years Dad's stock contemptuous response to any drama I reported about one of my friends was "at least he's not being hunted by the Russians," the litmus test of terror as he had experienced it.

White Eagle Over Wimbledon

This time he closed the argument sarcastically "Do you want to sell newspapers at the station with Montgomery?"

Jim's father was an American journalist. Dad threatened to tell the American Embassy Jim was a Communist.

Bluff or not, it shook James, who thought he might lose his U.S. passport and not be allowed to work in the United States. I remonstrated that the International Socialists who Jim belonged to were Trotskyites opposed to the Communist Party of Great Britain.

"I am not interested in squabbles within the English labour movement," he cut me short. And also "Why should I have to give those people my money?"

With rebellious Irish-American blood, James was a kindred anti-establishment spirit.

Boys with foreign blood looked after each other. As a 10-year-old I swung a punch at a boy who made fun of one of the few Jewish pupils at the school.

Intervention in favour of my friend provoked a stern speech by the headmaster of the junior school, Mr. Gibbs, in morning assembly.

"Gibby" told us that "You can't punch someone in the face just because you don't like something they've said." Fortunately my victim observed the schoolboy code against sneaking.

Later the whole school received a lecture from a visiting senior Royal Air Force officer, seeking to remind us on a recruiting drive, drawing on the lessons of the Korean War, about the constant dangers to the free world of the Communist threat.

After the lecture, Roderick Conway-Morris, a boy in the year above me who was an anarchist, raised a chortle miming a prisoner's posture, hopping with his hands over his head past the prefects at the Hall entrance.

The school history conceded that Shaw "was less successful in his efforts to solve the problems of Assembly ... he made several experiments, always retaining some element of prayer, but neither he nor the Chaplain could satisfy those who on the one hand shrank from orthodoxy, on the other were more concerned with positive support of anti-Establishment doctrines."

This echoed a debate about the school raging since its inception. King's was founded by the Duke of Wellington, Robert Peel and Archbishop Howley in response to the founding of University College, London. King's was to have no religious entry test and be open to all.

One of Wellington's chief political opponents was George Finch-Hatton, the 9th Earl of Winchelsea and Nottingham – a staunch defender of Protestantism, especially hostile to Catholic emancipation. He argued King's should be limited to those professing Anglicanism.

He charged Wellington with insincerity in his support for an Anglican King's College. Wellington, a supporter of the

White Eagle Over Wimbledon

Catholic Relief Act, felt the accusations were so serious to himself and King's that he sought satisfaction in arms.

The duel took place at 8 am on Saturday March 21, 1829. The Duke shot wide. The Earl shot in the air deliberately and had already presented an apology to the Duke.

"Wellington had defended the right to change the constitution as well as the rights of his College," an old boys' bulletin said, "the principles he defended are alive today – and the independence of King's College/King's College School to offer an education to all was secured."

An annual Duel Day dinner is held in Lambeth Palace to commemorate the duel's anniversary.

Occasional spats started by Dad with our rebellious public school friends and their parents were in a sense a luxury at the end of a long hard search for well being by someone who described himself as "a poor immigrant" when he arrived in England.

When Mum and Dad bought their first home in Camberley it was typical of Polish former servicemen settling in Britain.

"The pattern of getting a job and saving up the first months' pay-packets for the down payment on a mortgage lay at the root of … future well being, if not their prosperity," Zamoyski wrote.

"One fighter pilot married a girl from the Northolt area, got a job, and bought a house with a view of the airfield, in which he brought up three sons to be good Poles."

Dad by his example also did a great job of demonstrating good Polish values. Unfortunately I wasn't always very receptive, catching on quicker to Polish vices.

Zamoyski added perceptively that it was difficult to get Polish servicemen "in Britain to say anything other than that the British have been wonderful friends and allies. This does not stem from servility or from delusion, but from a remarkably cool appraisal of the realities of war and peace, and a warm appreciation of the deep and enduring friendship they did find here."

Close to the headmaster's study at King's hung a portrait of Dante Gabriel Rosetti, the painter, poet and founder of the pre-Raphaelite movement who taught Italian at the school.

Sitting near me in Frank Miles' panelled classroom with a view over the playing fields and tennis courts was the tall, gangly figure of Gabor (to us always 'Gaby') Rado. His father was Hungarian. He always seemed older than anyone in our year.

Gaby regaled us with anecdotes about life in Transylvania. He later became a well-known correspondent of Channel 4 news. Born in Budapest, he came to England when he was eight.

Clive Aslet, a civilised connoisseur of the arts, was a protégé of Frank who became a household name as editor of Country Life and a defender of English rural life.

White Eagle Over Wimbledon

Both men, like Conway-Morris, were earmarked for Cambridge. Frank looked after us in the top English set. He had the gift of making every boy think he was special.

"He has obvious intelligence and rare sensitivity," he wrote in my fifth form report. (average age of form 14.11. Age of boy 14.5). Another time he made my day returning an essay saying "yes, you've got a kind of natural style of writing."

My future was mapped, however, by Frank's formidable rival, the bearded head of history, Geoffrey Taylor.

Mr Taylor told us that still today in England everyone was either a roundhead or a cavalier. He went around the class dubbing all pupils royalists or puritans. "Phillips is a Cavalier ..."

Geoff also ran the school's voluntary service effort. Bored of bird watching, I began voluntary social work, visiting an orphanage in Mitcham with Tim Vaughan, a friend who played saxophone and whose father was a prominent arts broadcaster.

The orphanage director boasted of wartime deeds. Tim told him we had an Italian friend at school, Robin Bibi, a gifted musician, who formed a renowned blues band.

"I might have killed his father," the director said. "I hope I did."

Geoff's gentle coaching in the History Upper VIth as he filled the classroom with smoke from his pipe bore fruit.

Mr Shaw, my headmaster, stopped by one afternoon on his way to his nearby house to tell us I had won an Exhibition to University College, Oxford.

Not all my friends were lucky. Richard Court was an engaging, sensitive Charterhouse boy who dropped out of school after going to India on the hippie trail. He lived in a cottage off the Ridgeway with his mother, one of the few boys whose parents were divorced.

I spent many an enjoyable afternoon getting blasted with Richard and David Jones, who followed me to University College, at the home of Jonathan Tubbs where he lived with his architect father near Wimbledon Common.

After failing for Oxford, Richard drifted into dead-end clerical jobs in the Civil Service in part to finance drugs. One day he vanished. His body some weeks later was fished out of the Thames.

David McGladdery, a talented student and roustabout whose father was an Evening Standard journalist, had a promising future ahead of him as a historian or political scientist.

Writing essays for the British Constitution A level exam at the back of the school gym, a screwed up piece of paper hit my desk. I looked up to see McGladdery nodding vigorously.

"What the fxxx are the powers of the prime minister?" My suggestion tossed back to him may have helped obtain a

White Eagle Over Wimbledon

good grade. I last saw "Deeg," during a break he took from work as a labourer on the North Sea Oil Rigs.

Jim Montgomery took up his radical cudgels at the London School of Economics. He got caught up with some hardline London sympathisers of the Irish Republican movement.

Jim later returned to university to study law, qualified as a barrister and became a respectable American citizen, settling in New York.

The musician Jim Payne, took up hang gliding, was killed when his aircraft collapsed in mid air tumbling him to his death Daedalus style.

Many Wimbledonians also were ill equipped to live elsewhere. Forty years later I caught up with Jonathan Tubbs at the Rose and Crown pub near the Common.

Many old King's friends still live in the area or have returned to retire there, like old Imperial civil servants returning from India to die 'at home'.

Men like Tim Vaughan, James Dacie, William Armstrong, Morgan Tucker and the street-fighting Jones brothers all lived or retained a base in Wimbledon once again. Part of me was envious of them living in the familiar streets.

Jonathan and his wife Lucy lived in fashionable Marriott road, having only left Wimbledon for a couple of years in bohemian Battersea during decades of married life.

They were already going out together when they

attended my party at our house in Belvedere Drive when we were teenagers.

King's provided a strong basis for prosperity for men like Jonathan, whose father was a famous architect. He has his own successful architectural practise in Wimbledon.

Our religious education in Wimbledon's churches was another precious legacy. Many times in Catholic churches in Rome or in war zones around the world I have recalled standing by my father as a small boy early on Sunday in the almost empty Church of Christ the King, in Wimbledon Park, hearing Mass said in Polish.

Family reception for my parents' wedding vow renewal, left to right: Uncle John, Mrs Males, Aunt Jessie, Dr Kelly, Diana, John, Col. Delaveaux, Mum, Dad, Wimbledon's Polish parish priest.

White Eagle Over Wimbledon

Mum and Dad married in a registry office in 1950. Dad was 25 and Mum was 23. A Church wedding then would have been a luxury and anathema for the Catholic Church, since Mum was an Anglican. In Wimbledon, perhaps in part out of gratitude for their recent prosperity, they decided to renew their wedding vows in the Church of Christ the King.

A group photo from that renewal of vows service on the lawn at the back of our house, providing a record of different strands of our cross section of the Anglo-Polish community.

Beaming at the camera Dad looked cheerful, Mum ecstatic in a pink dress and Diana in matching pink frock, next to me, looking embarrassed, in a suit.

Also there were Uncle John and Aunt Jessie, Gen. de Laveaux, our spiritual guide the Polish priest from Christ the King, our cleaning lady, Mrs Males, and Dr Kelly.

Brigadier De Laveau died in 1972. Dad and I went to the funeral at Ealing cemetery with a crowd of old soldiers.

From time to time, Dad or one of the general's former subordinates stood up, rigidly at attention, remaining standing as a mark of respect, during the solemn rites. Then the coffin at last slid down into the crematorium fire on a chute beneath a rather macabre trap door in a corner of the chapel.

In his homily the priest recalled how, as a young man Ludwik had played a dramatic role in Pilsudski's legions in

Lwow in the front line of the fighters who revived Poland out of the ashes of the First World War.

Mrs de Laveaux, a minute grey-haired figure with high cheek bones, offered sherry at a subdued wake in their small flat. Her life was a struggle from then on. The British Government meanly decided Polish soldiers and their widows should not receive military pensions.

Chapter 8:
The Universal Blow

"The English-Polish combination produces fine children, solid British phlegm allied to Polish fantasy." Andrew Kowerski[42]

To find out more about my Polish, and English, roots, I immersed myself in history. In 1972, as we swotted for the Oxford entrance exam in Geoff Taylor's classroom overlooking the sloping village green lined with chestnut trees in front of the Hand in Hand pub, Dad gave me one of the best books about the Warsaw Uprising, written by former UPI journalist George Bruce.

Poland was way off the history curriculum in English schools. Essays from the time that survived in my old European history folder include such abstruse subjects as "Why did Charles V succeed in Spain but not in Germany?" – not one of my best efforts. The master marking commented that "you give the impression that you are dying to finish."

The architects of the history 'A' level syllabus evidently felt aspiring historians had little need at that stage of further information about a remote wartime ally in the much more recent past.

I read and re-read Bruces' book, looking for clues to that nature of Dad's life as a young teenage soldier. As a child he learned that for Poles occupation was nothing new.

The ancient Polish kingdom that as late as 1648 stretched from the Baltic almost to the Black Sea vanished in the three partitions of the late 18th century, re-emerged as a republic in 1918, and sunk once more at the fourth partition of September 1939.

One section in Bruce caught my attention. "Like many Poles, Bor Komorowski had a passion for 'good conspiratorial practice' - false identity documents, disguise, daily changes of rendezvous in homes of sympathisers to whom they were complete strangers; a new password every day, a different sleeping-place every night, and a tiny phial of cyanide for staff who knew the movement's secrets to swallow when all seemed lost."

The rising mastermind, Gen. Rowecki, wrote that "The uprising must be preceded by a long period of preparation, precise and detailed, followed by a violent, universal, synchronised blow, which, by staking all on one card by acting extraordinarily boldly should bring about a decisive solution after a few hours ..."

White Eagle Over Wimbledon

The blow was to be launched "when Germany was at its weakest and the Soviets too weak or disorganised to clamp their iron hand on the country," Bruce explained.

Home Army units, including one led by my father's commanding officer, Col. Kazimierz Tumidajski, (codename General Marcin), were fighting on the eve of the outbreak of the Warsaw Uprising in the Lublin district some 140 miles southeast of Warsaw.

They captured several small towns and destroyed a number of heavy enemy tanks and self-propelled guns.

Lublin was liberated by combined Home Army and Red Army forces July 22, 1944. Col. Tumidajski was a veteran of the Polish legions like Col. De Laveaux. He died in a Soviet prison hospital in 1947.

At its height, the AK in the Lublin region had around 1000 officers and reserves in its ranks. One of the most famous officers, Maj. Hieronim Dekutowski, *Zapora*, parachuted into the region. He had been in the field since 1939 having fought in the September war.

Blackwell says that a number of air drops by the RAF provided weapons for the Home Army in Lublin. When Dad's *Kmicic* unit was disarmed by the Red army near Majdan Forest on July 24, 1944, it handed in 36 semi-automatic LKMs, 6 grenades and a lot of ammunition.

I was gripped by Bruce's description of young men like my father. "Weapons apart, success in these conditions depended greatly on the capabilities, courage and leadership of junior commanders," he said.

"On those levels the Poles proved themselves superior. In the first days of the Uprising, before the arrival of German reinforcements, their aggression, resilience and speedy action enabled them to outweigh the heavy armament as well as the rigidity of the German military hierarchy."

"Polish junior commanders too often lost their lives owing to courage or impetuosity amounting to foolhardiness; but when one fell another spontaneously replaced him."

Zamoyski's study of the Polish Air Force became my bible about men like Uncle John. A bomber pilot is quoted as summing up the malaise that affected many such fliers.

The war "demoralized you for the rest of your life, because you had to accept the fact that life was not important and that, provided you survived, you could stuff the rest," the pilot, Zbigniew Bobiński said.

"You had to force yourself to think of everything as here today, gone tomorrow; some kind of instinct of self-preservation dictated that you shouldn't take anything too seriously …"

"So when, later, you came up against the ambition and competitiveness that are part of any career, you couldn't really be bothered; you did enough to be able to bring home enough money, and that was all. Some drank themselves to pieces."

White Eagle Over Wimbledon

I wondered if Uncle John in his heyday, courting Aunt Jessie in Scotland, before he began drinking himself to pieces, savoured the celebrity Zamoyski described Polish airmen enjoying.

"Word got out that Poles were good lovers, and young and unattached ladies in London felt they had to try one out. The airmen took up the challenge and enjoyed themselves, but did sometimes tire of the social whirl, and many were unhappy about being patronized."

A similar theme of coping with condescension was taken up by George Mikes in How to be an Alien, which he wrote teasingly was "a shame and bad taste" in England.

"There are some noble English people who might forgive you. There are some magnanimous souls who realise that it is not your fault, only your misfortune."

"They will invite you to their homes. Just as they keep lap-dogs and other pets, they are quite prepared to keep a few foreigners."

In our year off before university I spent two months tramping around the Lot and the Loire regions in France together with James Dacie including a stay at the idyllic Montgomery holiday home, a converted barn, in the Dordogne.

We found James Montgomery riding around the countryside on his motorbike, striking fear into British expats in the bars in the area or driving a tractor with the farmers. At one point he was stricken with sunstroke and became delirious.

On our way through Brittany James and I tried our hands at rock climbing on some of the huge boulders littering parts of the Breton coast. One climb provided the source for a lifelong nightmare.

I threw myself into the ascent of one 80 foot high rock without troubling to look for the safest way to the summit. Some 60 feet up I became stuck like a fly on a wall, blocked by an overhanging ledge. I could see no way of passing.

Fortunately James had taken the trouble to find the most intelligent route to the top from the other side of the rock. Answering my cries for help he came down from the summit to a point diagonally close to the overhanging ledge and was able to spot handholds that I had missed and guide me up to safety with a final tug of my wrist.

I would never race up a rockface like that again. Time and time again over the subsequent 40 years at times of stress I have endured anguished cauchemars of being stuck on a window ledge at a great height with the window closed or barely open.

These are dreams that from early experiences I can only relate to the time James saved me from tumbling onto the rocky Breton shore to meet a similar end to Jim Payne.

Our love for France nurtured during that long trip was for me one step closer to Poland to be nourished and followed by a passion for Italy and penetration into the

White Eagle Over Wimbledon

hospitable Slavic world in ex Yugoslavia. I immediately felt at home among the artistic Slovenes.

In touch with American culture through his father, a correspondent for the U.S. network NBC, James had a fund of amusing Polack jokes from across the Atlantic. When we were together he would imitate my father's choicer Army slang phrases in an exaggerated foreign accent.

Unsurprisingly "you move like a fly in shit" and "he thought they were going to cut off his prick," were his favourites. Fortunately James was equally unforgiving of Irish and Americans.

Dad only had a very slight accent. His English was fluent and like many Slavs he was a polyglot, speaking Portuguese, Spanish, Russian and German as well as French and Italian. On business trips to Germany he prudently never disclosed that he was a Pole.

I recall being impressed as he rattled out fluent German to chat up an attractive German woman in a bikini lying next to us on the beach during a family holiday at Sitges.

One night he had a tiff with Mum. In a furious mood he took me to a night club where we watched Flamenco dancers into the night. Dad would practise his Portuguese, also, during the long drives down to Santos from Sao Paolo.

In German company, at least, Dad's undercover identity continued. It was hard to believe such a gentleman could have ever been ruthless enough to be a spy or to kill.

John Phillips

"I hope I didn't kill anyone," he once said, a comment that reassured me but also was vaguely disappointing. Instead Dad inculcated me with the idea that one should always be ready for the worst, armed with the requisite weapons to use, reluctantly, if necessary.

Sketch of Anna De Laveaux by Italian prisoner in German POW camp

Chapter 9:
Poles of perception

"My father was a wartime spy," I told the man from MI6 as we ate at a Rome restaurant. "He won a Polish Military Cross."

"Well, how wonderful. Why don't you get the citation?" In fact there was no Polish military cross, as far as I have been able to determine. Its existence was probably another family myth like Uncle John having been on the last Polish Air Force plane to leave Warsaw or being in the Battle of Britain.

This friend working in British Intelligence told me how much he admired his Polish counterparts after the fall of communism. But not all Poles admired people like me.

"You are not Polish," a young Pole I ran into in Kensington a few years ago told me bluntly. One of the wave of "plumbers" who swept into the UK when Poland joined the EU, he was working in a café near Imperial College. "Your father was Polish but you are English."

For that tough young Pole, Polish identity was not a birthright to be claimed by any Tom, Dick or Harry who happened to be born to a Polish parent in England and lived a cushy life. Thanks a lot.

Yet Poland had been an abstract idea for some famous Polish exiles including Adam Mickiewicz, the national poet of Poland.

"Mickiewicz, sent into exile at the age of 24, never visited the country we now know as Poland at all, apart from a brief foray into Prussian-occupied Poland near Poznan during the insurrection of 1830-1," Neil Ascherson wrote.

"He never saw either Warsaw or Krakow, the two capital cities of historic Poland. It is as if Shakespeare had been an Anglo-Irishman brought up in Dublin, driven to take refuge in Paris before he could find his way to London." [43]

The spooky friend might have materialised out of another book that Dad gave me with a meaningful look.

The present he bought for me in the wonderful, musty second-hand book shop in Wimbledon High Street, was A history of the Secret Service, by Richard Deacon, who served with Ian Fleming in naval intelligence.

Deacon examined the death of General Sikorski, the Polish Prime Minister who was killed mysteriously when the aircraft he was flying in crashed after taking off from Gibralter.

Deacon wrote that "the issue has been unecessarily complicated by dragging in Churchill's name without an iota of evidence to link Churchill personally with the incident."

White Eagle Over Wimbledon

More important, he said, was Hochhuth's other allegation that General MacFarlane knew in advance of British plans to kill the Polish C.-in-C. and that he warned Sikorski and his daughter against flying in the Liberator bomber in which they crashed.

The Governor suggested that Sikorski should travel in another plane in which M. Maisky, the Soviet Ambassador to London, was going to Cairo.

General Kukiel, Minister of Defence in the Polish Government in exile, confirmed both MacFarlane's warning to Sikorski not to travel in the Liberator and the suggestion that he should go in Maisky's plane.

The Governor repeated the warning three times.

The warnings "caused grave displeasure in the Secret Service hierarchy and angered Churchill so much that he refused to speak to MacFarlane, cutting him dead on the steps of a London club when the two men met face to face," said Deacon.

"The British Foreign Office and Service Ministries have consistently refused information to writers on the subject, particularly on the identity of the two Secret Servicemen who were supposed to be on the plane, but whose bodies were never recovered and who were said to have left the plane before the crash."

Some right-wing Poles wanted Sikorski out of the way. Previous sabotage attempts were made on his aircraft, one with an incendiary device.

Admiral Guy Guant, a friend of Macfarlane, was convinced the governor suspected an attempt at sabotage, that MacFarlane had been tipped off from Tangier.

"This was the reason for his warnings," he told Deacon, "I don't think MacFarlane had any details whatsoever of the plot, but he was particularly disturbed because he could not be sure who was behind it."

"He suspected that it had been planned from Tangier and that British intelligence in Tangier had failed to warn Gibralter. He was extremely angry that the Intelligence Department in Gibralter pooh-poohed the idea."

The book was at any rate essential on the reading list for a son to be prepared for the underground life.

John Le Carré echoed Deacon. "For those who enjoy tortuous speculation, there is one intriguing coincidence," he wrote. "Sikorski, whose assassination Rolf Hochhuth notoriously attributes to Winston Churchill, took off from Gibralter on July 4, 1943."

"At that time Kim Philby was in charge of SIS counter-intelligence operations on the Iberian peninsula. If Sikorsky was assassinated, is it conceivable that Philby planned the operation on behalf of his Russian masters, and that his assassin whom he hired believed he was working for the British?" [44]

Missing the lively British Club we had enjoyed in Brazil, Dad joined the RAC country club where I carried golf clubs

White Eagle Over Wimbledon

for him, the RAC in London and the Hurlingham Club in Putney where the swimming pool also recalled the outdoor life that had been exhilarating in Latin America. The Hurlingham with its polo field was exclusive, providing Diana with attention from many old Etonians frequenting its disco.

Dad proposed as a member John Radcliffe, a doctor from a London teaching hospital who lived on Wimbledon Hill. His daughter Dominique was Diana's best friend. Our families had a joint holiday one year in Tunisia, starting my fascination with the Arab world.

Reading by the pool in Sfax, I began searching out perceptions of Poles in English literature. The Mask of Dimitrios by Eric Ambler was a favourite of Dad's that I read.

In another gripping Ambler thriller, The Nightcomers, the hero is an unassuming English engineer whose wife left him for a Polish Army officer while he was doing war service.

Spotting Dad's copy of The Spy who Came in from the Cold led me to make the acquaintance of Leiser, in Le Carré's Looking Glass War, an entertaining but in some ways pathetic Polish former secret agent who British Intelligence reluctantly takes out of mothballs for undercover work:

"What kind of man was he?" Leclerc persisted.[45]

"Common, in a Slav way. Small. He plays the Rittmeister. It's most unattractive."

"He dresses like a bookie, but I suppose they all do that … we spoke about politics. He's not that sort of exile. He considers himself integrated, naturalized British."

Such remarks confirmed Mikes' opinion in How to be an Alien: "The verb *to naturalise* clearly proves what the British think of you. Before you are admitted to British citizenship you are not even considered a natural human being."

Even Leiser's louche English girlfriend berates him after he is approached to re-join British Intelligence:

"… well, who was it?"

"He's from one of the big companies."

"And they want you?"

"Yes … they want to make me an offer."

"Christ, who'd want a bloody Pole?"

A film of the novel released in 1969 starred Christopher Jones as Leiser and Ralph Richardson as LeClerc. Leiser was recast in the movie as a handsome young defector.

Anthony Powell was the first British author to explore the Katyn massacre in his 1968 novel, The Military Philosophers, based on his time serving as a liason officer with Polish forces.

Powell gave an insight into the reaction of British army top brass at the Ministry of Defence when the mass graves of Polish officers were discovered at Katyn. Comic villain,

White Eagle Over Wimbledon

Kenneth Widmerpool has little patience with the Polish London Government.

"In any case," said Widmerpool, "whatever materializes, even if it does transpire – which I sincerely trust it will not – that the Russians behaved in such a very regrettable manner, how can this country possibly raise official objection, in the interests of a few thousand Polish exiles, who, however worthy their cause, cannot properly handle their diplomatic relations, even with fellow Slavs?" [46]

Not all British officers at the MOD meeting depicted by Powell were so unfeeling.

"The Soldier, youngish with a slight stutter, who looked like a Regular, shook his papers together and put them into a briefcase."

"It's quite a crowd," he said.

"What are the actual figures?" asked the sailor.

"Been put as high as nine or ten thousand," said the airman.

"… you can't exactly blame them for making enquires through the International Red Cross," the soldier insisted.

Britain's attitude to Katyn featured in Robert Harris's novel, Enigma, about the code-breakers who developed the Enigma machine, provided to Britain by Polish Intelligence.

The villain is Pukowski, nickname "Puck," a Polish codebreaker who turns traitor when he discovers Britain turned a blind eye to information about Katyn, whose victims included his father.

Wigram, an intelligence officer, explains to the book's hero, mathematician Tom Jericho, the thinking behind British silence.

"Stalin's the biggest enemy Hitler's got, so as far as we're concerned, for present purposes, he's a bloody good friend of ours. Katyn massacre? Katyn frigging massacre? Thanks awfully, but, really, do shut up."

"I don't suppose Puck would have seen it quite like that."

"Shall I tell you something? I think he rather hated us. After all, if it hadn't been for the Poles we might not even have broken Enigma in the first place. But the people he really hated were the Russians. And he was prepared to do anything to get revenge. Even if it meant helping the Germans."

Unsurprisingly the Polish community in Britain took umbrage at Harris's plot.

Jan Ciechanowski, a distinguished historian, wrote that "In view of the Polish achievements in breaking the Enigma and defending the Ultra secrets, to present a Pole as a traitor in a work of fiction but set against the background of such an historical event, seem a very shabby and unfair treatment."

Spy authors Len Deighton and Ted Allbeury also explored the figures of the Anglo-Pole and the Polish-Scot (or Scots-Pole).

White Eagle Over Wimbledon

Deighton's *Hope* (1995) introduces George Kosinski, brother-in-law of Bernard Samson, an SIS master spy who, like the young Pole I met in Kensington, disparages those who are not real Poles but only "consider themselves such."

"George was Polish by extraction and a Londoner by birth. He was not handsome or charming but he was direct in manner and unstinting in his generosity," Deighton wrote.

"Many of the men he did deals with, and the ones who sat alongside him on his charity committees, were Poles, or considered themselves as such." [47]

George is lured to spy for the Polish Communist Government, in order to keep control of his family estates. Samson brings him back to England from Poland.

"Come home, George. Come and tell us all you know," Samson tells him. "You're a Londoner, you're not Polish. Forget all this crap they've been feeding you."

Bernard hands George to the British, remarking "He thought he'd found a home in Poland but he hasn't got a home anywhere. It's tough ..."

Allbeury painted a truer figure in *The Judas Factor*.[48]

"Tadeusz Charles Anders was a big-built man, but his six feet one inch made his broad shoulders look less broad and made his face look less aggressive ... Those who looked carefully at faces would have said that it wasn't an English face. And they would have been right. His father had been

Polish and his mother a Scot, and the sets of flamboyant genes showed not only in his face but in his temperament."

"There was no doubt that the Polish genes were dominant, and they and a few other factors in his early life had been responsible for his troubles in SIS. They valued and used his physical strength, even his wild outbreaks of anger when provoked. But as an established officer of SIS they saw him as a potential source of embarrassment."

"He still worked for them, and it was SIS cash that had funded the setting up of his club. As an undercover man he was invaluable."

Anders' father had been killed at Monte Cassino. Tad joined the Coldstream Guards and found his way to SIS.

SIS took him off its official payroll and gave him an undercover job running a Soho club after he tore the intestines out of a Soviet spy who raped his girlfriend.

"He was useful but dangerous, and that was the end of it for them. But they showed no embarrassment when they briefed him to do the things that went against their grain, and he sensed that they no longer even considered him to be an Englishman."

The book opens with a girlfriend of Anders asking:

"*Are* you a Jew, Charles?" The Man didn't look up as he filled his own glass slowly and carefully.

"No, what made you ask?"

"Daddy says you are in his letter." She quotes her father: "I wonder how you could be so easily deceived by this man.

White Eagle Over Wimbledon

You make him out to be some sort of Sir Galahad. I see him more as a typical central European, Jew-boy entrepreneur ..."

Allbeury captures well the suspicion of some of establishment Britain for Poles, attitudes I would encounter at the *Times*, where enemies whispered that those of Eastern European origin like Anatol Levin, a Latvian prince, and myself, must be Jews.[49]

Allbeury took up the theme again in *The Special Collection*. Stephen Felinski is a wealthy spy whose family settled in England as refugees from the 1830 Polish uprising.

After a good war, Felinski found it hard fitting into Britain. "Large organizations looked at the tough young man who came to interviews. They liked the DSO, but they didn't like the private income."

"They couldn't categorize the man who had been to Harrow and Christ Church, whose English was better than theirs, yet went with a name like Felinski. Although the Polish origins went back 100 years they found it disturbing. Some were interested enough to ask where Poland was." [50]

George Steiner wrote from another angle in *Sweet Mars*. Gerald Maune meets Jan, a Polish liason officer in the Western Desert, in a Cairo military hospital as they recover from wounds. Maune has a homo erotic adventure with Jan, who had "night-blue" eyes, "pitch-black hair" and "moved down the ward like a fencer." [51]

Steiner portrayed Poles as revenge obsessed. "He was the first man I met who thought of it in that way, who had a personal war. He said that whenever he could, he shot low, so that they would feel themselves die."

But I am getting ahead of myself. As a very young student reading history at Oxford I was attracted by aspects of Marxist ideology, through Marxian theories of economics.

I eventually drew back, however, from dogmatic left-wing ideas when a close university friend, David Clifford, a brilliant philosophy student, recommended me Karl Popper's demolition of fallacious Marxist claims to a "scientific" theory of historical development.

"Read that," David said firmly, "or perhaps you don't want to."

David's mother and grandfather had been prisoners of the Japanese and his father fought with the British army in Burma.

Inducted into a London fast lane while working as a labourer in Notting Hill Gate, he proved a kind mentor when I went up to the university aged 17, the youngest student in my college year.

Over many glasses of whiskey in the early hours as the clock struck in University College quad near the monument to Shelley, the College's most famous alumnus, I listened to David's account of his upbringing in Indonesia and India recognising a family odyssey at least as colourful as ours.

White Eagle Over Wimbledon

Dad visited the digs we shared in Osney near Oxford Canal and the beautiful Port Meadow in our third year, amusing David by annotating a careers advice brochure we had been puzzling over with emphatic comments on what he viewed as futile job options: "bullshit!" was his frequent comment.

College elections provided a bizarre insight into communist tactics. Under the guidance of the only member of the Communist Party at Univ., electoral officials connived with a candidate for JCR president to stuff ballot boxes and ensure his election. Another candidate who was high on LSD as he delivered his electoral speech ended up in a mental hospital and dropped out of Oxford.

Periodically other friends and acquaintances would become interested in my Polish background though few realised how much it meant to me. What had started as a source of surprise and even bewilderment became a font of great pride, perhaps too much so given how little I had been willing to find out more about Polish language and culture as a boy.

Bruce described how Polish insurgents escaped through Warsaw's sewers.

The description reminded me of the evening Mum and I had watched the Wajda film *Kanal* on our tiny black and white television set.

"Everything depended upon the speed with which they stumbled the four kilometres through the sewage to the City

Centre, for the truce ended at dawn," wrote Bruce, "Four hours were reckoned the shortest possible time, each man holding on to the one ahead ... many could not go on and fell unconscious in the stream of sewage."

As one expert noted "Sewer was the very first portrayal of *The Rising* on screen. It was passed by the censors probably because it depicted the searing tragedy of the insurgents, and by implication the futility of their sacrifice."

"Yet the film's effect did not match the censors' expectations. The scene which everyone remembered was the one where a group of desperate survivors, wading through the effluent, reach an exit grille on the bank of the Vistula, and gaze in dying frustration at the far side of the river. No one watching the film could fail to realize who had been occupying the right bank of the Vistula in September 1944 or what they had done."

Turning to a psychiatrist later when I was suffering from depression, I told him of a nightmare I had in which I watched helplessly as my two daughters sank without trace into the water of a canal.

The psychiatrist was certain the canal was a sewer from *The Rising* embedded in my subconscious.

In 2001 the Mainstream Press published in English one of the most vivid accounts of the uprising.

By Devil's Luck, by Stanislaw Likiernik brings out the heroism and the suicidal odds facing the fighters as one

White Eagle Over Wimbledon

after another of Likiernik's friends from the elite Kedew battalion are killed.

Likiernik and a comrade with the alias Colombus were models for the character Stanislaw Skiernik in a novel, *Kolumbowie Rocznik 20* (Columbus Vintage 1920).

Written by Roman Bratny, a pseudonym of Roman Mularczyk, it was the first publication in Communist Poland daring to present the non-Communist Underground positively.

Likiernik concludes his memoir with lessons. "Never be afraid, fear is a bad counsel. And my final and most important lesson: liberty is to be valued over anything else, life without freedom is intolerable."

"… Nothing shall erase from my memory the exhilaration of resistance with weapons in one's hands, of bringing the fight to the enemy."

One of the first people I met in Beirut was Andrew Borowiec, a Polish American journalist. He had been a boy soldier in the Warsaw Uprising, fighting at age 15. His memoir, 'Warsaw Boy,' a superlative account of the insurrection, brings the drama alive even more graphically than Likiernik.

As a war correspondent I felt I must be braver than my colleagues to honour my Polish origins. I believed there was a fund of courage in my genes into which I could tap.

Chapter 10: The Castle

> *"A large number of Polish patriots risked their lives to get out of Poland and make their way to Great Britain ... they brought to heterosexuality an enthusiasm which was sometimes excessive."*
> Rebecca West, *The Meaning of Treason*[52]

When I returned to England from study in Italy, our Belvedere Drive idyll reproducing the life of Polish gentry was over. The big family home had been sold for a more modest one in Spencer Hill, an artery street that winds down the Wimbledon hillside from the Ridgeway, a former Roman sheep track, to Worple road near the river Wandle.

Soaring council rates meant the only way to stay in Bellver House would have been to rent out a wing. We could have lived comfortably in half the building, as we did for periods while renovation work was under way. Mum wouldn't contemplate living cheek by jowl with tenants, however.

Dad began all over again, reproducing the forests of his youth from the foothills of the Tatra mountains, planting conifer trees at the smaller garden in Spencer Hill. This time he would not see them flourish.

By the time we moved to Spencer Hill, my parents' relationship could be said to have become somewhat fraught.

As a post-graduate student in Florence at the newly founded European University Institute (EUI), I made friends with a bohemian Slovene student, Emil. His southern Slav mannerisms often recalled the Poles.

"I wouldn't have someone like that in my unit," Dad muttered, "I would send him in the front line to get shot."

He was scathing about latter day Yugoslavs in general, arguing that King Petar of Yugoslavia had been betrayed by the communists.

"I would never have given up my weapons to Tito," he mused. He surmised that I was largely wasting time in Florence. "You'll never get a job in England with your attitudes."

Italy surpassed my expectations raised by Dad's accounts of his adventures with the Anders Army during the war. The European University was relaxed in the first year of its existence. My French supervisor tolerated the slow progress I made on my Ph. D.

Silvia, an Italian student in Polish history whose father was a Corriere della Sera journalist, took me under her wing, one of the first of several Florentine girlfriends. "Ireneusz!" she said, "a very aristocratic name."

The attraction was instant. Pursuing it was irregular but everything seemed permitted in those heady first weeks of the first pan-European university.

We dreamed of rebuilding Europe according to libertarian rules. Soon Silvia was calling her husband to explain why she was staying out for a feverish night. Had I become as bad as Mirek?

Students at the institute had semi-diplomatic status but nevertheless I managed to get caught up in Italy's drama as Marxist terrorists sought to overthrow the state.

Climbing over a gate into a villa where another student lived one night, Wilson Finnie, a Scot studying law, and I, were arrested by suspicious Italian anti-terrorist police.

A group of Red Brigades terrorists had escaped from prison the same night and killed a police man. After being roughed up and passing a night in the cells and another in the somewhat grim Murate jail we were bailed out by the British Consul in Florence. It was a sobering experience about which, fortunately, Dad did not hear. Wilson appropriately went on to be Dean of the law faculty at Edinburgh university.

Back in England in 1979 I found Dad had become a bachelor living in a gloomy bedsitting flat in a nondescript street in North London.

Then there was an enjoyable spell he spent living in some style for a while in a smart flat in the posh Kensington end

White Eagle Over Wimbledon

of Earl's Court owned by his Polish general's widow, an area known once as the Polish Corridor. I had digs nearby at Kensington Gardens, shared with Giovanni, an amusing Italian remittance man, and would walk to Dad's flat in the warm summer evenings.

Worse was to follow as Dad was forced by his company to take early retirement from his job. Only in retrospect would I realise how much I took for granted my prosperous, happy childhood, with its spacious homes and gardens.

A writer from another Slav country, Ivo Andric, wrote poignantly, amidst the misery and tragedy of the Second World War, that "While creating a home is as difficult and slow as going uphill, the dismantling of an institution or a household goes as quickly and easily as a downhill path." [53]

In that period I often met my father with Diana, who had become the first woman to win a scholarship to study law at University College, Oxford, in the London Poles' favourite haunt at Daquise, the Polish restaurant in Kensington with wonderful pictures of the Uhlan lancers on the walls.

He found consolation, however, in the news that Poles were fighting off the Soviet yoke again with the birth of the Solidarity trade union Solidarnosc, a coalition of workers and intellectuals led by an electrician, Lech Walesa.

Dad took a flat in the smart end of Earl's Court near Gloucester Road in a posh block owned by the widow of his general (I never discovered which one). Since we had first moved to London in the early 60s the city had changed not necessarily for the better.

"Look at how these people drive," he remarked as he helped me move to my flat in nearby Kensington Gardens. "Too many foreigners!" he added.

"You no longer consider yourself a foreigner?" I asked.

"I've been here long enough," he retorted. "I've paid enough taxes."

Dad began working for the Polish-Government-in-Exile's office looking after Polish refugees who fled to Italy from martial law. Long derided as a group of elderly dreamers, the "ministers" at the government's Eaton Square, Belgravia, headquarters – known as *Zamek*, "The Castle" – who ranged in age from 61 to 80, had no difficulty in adjusting to the new atmosphere of hope.

Equally good news, bringing tears to Dad's eyes as he listened to the outcome in Rome with Diana, was the election in the conclave of 1978 of the Polish cardinal, Karol Wojtyla, to St. Peter's throne in the Vatican, where he became Pope John Paul II.

Earlier that year Wojtyla, then the Archbishop of Cracow, had told the ailing Pope Paul VI while visiting Rome to preach the Lenten sermons that "the game was up, that there should not be excessive worry about Communism because it was finished." [54]

White Eagle Over Wimbledon

Disillusioned with academic research, I had appalled my father once again by throwing up the generous scholarship at the European University to seek exciting work as a reporter. To escape the depressing home scene in Spencer Hill while my French girlfriend, Sylvie Richaud, from Florence was in London, I moved into a squat near Tower Bridge for a short while.

The squatters' leader was tough and impressive. "We have possession," he said after jemmying open a flat for us in Copperfield House on the Dickens Estate.

The neighbours included a group of 20 young Italians living on Social Security. I moved into basement digs in Islington after local people began firebombing squatters' cars. The episode provided me with material for my first published article, in the Evening Standard.

As a young journalist working for the BBC External Services I was criticised for "always reading the Morning Star," the British Communist daily newspaper.

I really only opened the odd newspaper to wind up some of the over-serious BBC editors such as Lesley Stone, a Thatcherite convert who eventually left the Corporation over his right-wing politics.

Roland Challis, the shrewd head of the Current Affairs Talks Department, indoctrinated me in some fundamentals of journalistic lore. "The first ten years of journalism are pretty insecure," he said. "It gets better after that."

John Phillips

John Phillips at work in the Wimbledon Guardian office, 1980.

From time to time I would visit the Bush House studios of the BBC Polish Service to seek advice from the elderly broadcasters hard at work there.

From those studios during the Second World War ingenious systems had been set up for using the BBC's overseas broadcasts as forewarnings that an RAF drop of arms would be made into occupied Poland. Particular tunes, played at 1:45 pm. after the news broadcast to Poland, meant drops to particular groups of fighters.

My BBC contract expired and I found myself covering the Polish community's attitude to events in Poland in the local newspaper in Wimbledon, the *South London Guardian*.

White Eagle Over Wimbledon

As the police and fire reporter for Tooting and Mitcham I enjoyed many pleasant lunches with Patricia, my female, posh, opposite number from the Wimbledon News in the pub facing Mitcham's sedate cricket green.

The *Guardian* owner, Paul Morgan, a former editor on the *Daily Express*, was an impressive entrepreneur who pretended to nourish a hatred for Oxford graduates.

The hard-nosed, hard-boozing Editor, Richard Felton, took our mission seriously and liked to recall his brother, a subaltern on active service in Northern Ireland.

"Look at this lazy effort. You could be leading a platoon in Ulster," he would say when admonishing me at the bar of the pub near the office for some minor inaccuracy in court or council coverage. Much of his advice to me at the bar was good. "There is no honour in newspapers," was one gem of Richard's that would prove true time and again through my career. But it was time to move on.

Putting my motorbike on the boat train to Paris and returning to Rome soon after the assassination attempt on the Pope in 1981, I cheered up Dad by writing about the Polish pope for the *Financial Times*.

I also worked night shifts at the Associated Press bureau to help meet the insatiable American newspaper appetite for stories about John Paul after he was shot and wounded in St. Peter's Square May 13, 1981.

Not long afterwards United Press International's gentlemanly foreign editor, Jack Payton, gave me a job as a staff correspondent in its Rome office after a friend in the office, Daniela Iacono, tipped me off that a job was opening up.

I became one of the fortunate reporters who followed John Paul in his travels around Italy and on the papal plane to Latin America and Europe.

Charles Ridley, a legendary UP journalist who had fought with the Poles as a captain in the British Army's 56th Reconnaissance regiment at Monte Cassino, took me under his wing. "He probably works for British intelligence," my father said when I told him about Charles.

On the contrary, I discovered, Charles was careful to keep his distance from spooks.

Charles's first posting was to Warsaw in 1950-51. Horrified by what he saw there, he wrote: "During my time in Warsaw, the Stalinist subjugation of the Polish nation was in its most gruesome early stages. The appalling reign of terror in that Russian-imposed police state sparked a personal crusade that pervaded my professional life." [55]

During the war he had developed a passion for Italy, and a Rome posting during the 1950s reinforced his love for the country.

The posting ended when he outraged UP executives by clambering on a table, unzipping his flies and declaring "I

White Eagle Over Wimbledon

piss on you Italians" at a dinner for honchos from ANSA, the Italian news agency.

Over numerous lunches we enjoyed at the old Foreign Press Club building in the Via della Mercede, Charles recounted some of his adventures with the Carpathian Lancers at Monte Cassino.

At the same time he debunked the notion that Polish troops were in some way supermen. "The choice of the Poles for the final assault was coincidental," he said, "it could have been done by English soldiers or any of the other nationalities involved."

Charles's wild streak continued in Paris where he earned fame for hurling a bar stool through the huge mirror in Harry's Bar, a watering hole for newsmen. I learned that the same fate had befallen the mirror at the *Associazione della Stampa Estera* in Rome.

In 1980 he had begun a 14-year assignment in Rome, at the start of what Charles described as "Polish Pope John Paul II's triumphant 10-year crusade to guide the overwhelmingly Catholic Poles in their successful bid to oust the hated Communist regime."

In the 1980s Rome was a front line in the Cold War with Italian and other investigators trying to prove the so-called "Bulgarian connection," to the attempt on the pope's life by Mehmet Ali Agca in St Peter's Square, May 13, 1981.

John Phillips

The shooting was frequently discussed at the Foreign Press Club bar. Among regulars was Christo Petrov, an engaging Bulgarian working for the BTA news agency.

Petrov wrote a book refuting allegations Bulgaria was behind the attack. However experts such as David Willey, the BBC Vatican reporter, remain convinced that Agca was working for the Bulgarian, and ultimately Soviet secret service. The Turkish terrorist fired six shots at the popemobile. The pope was hit four times, twice in the stomach.

"Chris Petrov has a strange reputation here," a well-informed Bulgarian journalist told me in Sofia. "Many people believe he planned the assassination attempt on the pope."

One night after a heavy session at the Club bar, Christo ended up at my apartment near the Campo di Fiori taking a nightcap. "John, do you know anyone in the English secret service?" he asked me, "I want to defect." I promised to pass the offer if I could, but said I knew British newspapers would pay well to learn the truth about the papal shooting.

Christo's English is masterly. As he staggered down the stairs of my apartment block he turned and said: "I'm not going to come clean mate."

Interviewing the pontiff at high altitude was almost as frightening as flying a Chipmunk 15 years earlier.

Dressed in white robes and a skullcap, John Paul strode back into the business class section to meet a jostling crowd of reporters.

White Eagle Over Wimbledon

Each correspondent, suitably fortified by a Bloody Mary mixed by *Time* magazine photographer, Rudi Frei, was given one shot at asking the pontiff a question as his Opus Dei press secretary, Joaquin Navarro-Valls, hovered protectively.

I managed at last what I hoped was a suitably weighty question about his Benelux pilgrimage. "Holy Father, do you think the Dutch Church is more or less united after your visit?"

There was a brief pause as the big plane streaked across the Alps. Then the pope replied enigmatically in accented Italian: "I don't know, but the country received the blessing of the apostle of the Holy Roman Catholic Church."

John Paul had done his duty by taking his mission to the unruly Dutch and so, for once, perhaps, had I.

Sadly my father did not live to hear me tell him about my encounter with the Poles', and Eastern Europe's, saviour.

Having been cast on the executive scrapheap as collateral damage by Unilever in the cruel cockpit of Thatcherite Britain, Dad died Nov. 5, 1984, from a stroke that hit him after he had been dancing at a reception at the Polish Club in Hammersmith. He was barely 60.

His death was devastating. My main personal feeling was guilt at not having devoted more time to helping him.

A dense crowd of Polish friends attended the funeral presided over by Fr. Gula, the kind parish priest from St. John's Polish Church in Putney who moved to London after working in the forefront of the Solidarity movement.

We buried Dad in the Polish section of a West London cemetery just five years before the re-birth of a free, independent Poland in the communist world's first free elections in 1989.

The funeral and burial were difficult. Mourners divided between those who supported my Mother and those who sympathised with his Polish girlfriend. Fr. Gula was a tower of strength in ensuring everything was done correctly.

In 1990 the Polish Government in Exile made its last significant act when it handed over the presidential insignia, guarded in London since the Second World War, to President Walesa.

Work by historians recently suggests that Uncle John may have got it right about many aspects of Britain's treatment of Poland.

Books like "For your freedom and ours" by Lynne Olsen and Stanley Cloud recount shabby treatment of the heroes of the Kościuszko squadron, RAF's ace 303 formation.

The performance of Polish pilots in the Battle of Britain alone could be said to have been decisive in the outcome of the war but their widows were denied a war pension.

Hugh Dowding said that "Had it not been for the magnificent [work] of the Polish squadrons and their unsurpassed gallantry, I hesitate to say that the outcome of battle would have been the same."

White Eagle Over Wimbledon

Interest in 303 Squadron revived in 2010 on the 70th anniversary of the Battle. Channel 4 produced a film about 303, "The Untold Battle of Britain," part of a series entitled "Bloody Foreigners."

In another manifest injustice, Gen. Stanislaw Macek, who led the Polish First Armoured Division that played a crucial part in routing the Wehrmacht at Falaise remained in Scotland but received no pension from the British. He worked as a barman in an Edinburgh hotel until the 1960s. Eventually the Dutch gave him a pension in honour of his liberation of Breda.

The thrilling turn of events in Poland in the early 80s had kept up my father's spirits when his fortunes ebbed. But in his last years he lost some of his faith in British society.

"Western democracy is only apparent," he went so far as to say once. And also, more sadly as he contemplated losing our family home, "at least we got your education right, John."

Mum disastrously sold our Spencer Hill home and moved into a flat near Wimbledon Common, then relocated to north London and was hospitalized while trying to move back to the north of England.

Diana began her career as an investment banker at Lazard Frères, however, wisely buying a flat in Hampstead.

And Father Gula, recovering from a stroke in his simple parish vestry near Putney Heath, kept up my spirits with encouragement to write books to make me independent of journalism.

"That is your treasure. If you write that book it will be good for you."

Fr. Gula bequeathed his own treasure to me when I read his history of the Polish Church in Britain.

His book was much more than just a history, encompassing a powerful investigation of the whole nature of Polish national identity and a defence of Polish nationalism.

Unusually for a Catholic priest, he candidly acknowledged the hostility that Pope Pius XII's "ambiguous" policies towards Nazi Germany engendered among Polish soldiers through the war.

His study traces the travails of the first Polish communities established in the UK after the 1830 Rising up to the 1930s when a Polish Mission was established by the Church in London.

Then, as now, "the imagination and openness of the Poles, their readiness to 'work hard and play hard' together with their generosity won them many friends," Fr Gula wrote.

"However, no doubt this annoyed certain people of a different culture and even caused jealousy."

Most Poles by the 1960s and 70s had integrated so well in Britain that "nobody noticed them."

White Eagle Over Wimbledon

Polish patriotism, he notes, was accompanied by an ethical code dating to the crusading belief that Poland was a chosen nation with a mission to defend Christianity that climaxed when Polish knights defeated the Turks at Vienna in 1683.

John working for UPI, Spanish Steps, Rome

Chapter 11: Tidying up history

"As for Butterworth, Adam thought as he walked across the park, what did he know about the Green Line? What the hell?"
James Buchan, *A Parish of Rich Women*[56]

"Filipowicz, Filipowicz!"

Juan Carlos Gumucio, a friend and outstanding war correspondent with whom I worked in Rome, Algiers and Beirut, was a great admirer of the Poles. As a somewhat subversive Bolivian he liked to think of me as a fellow outsider.

JC would hail me from the bar of the Commodore Hotel in Beirut as I walked in off the tough streets I had crossed from the UPI office in Hamra. "Filipowicz, Filipowicz!"

Looking down the sights of an AK 47 assault rifle with a group of militiamen and Juan Carlos outside the Commodore or running for cover in my bathroom when the hotel came under artillery fire, I felt I was surely upholding family traditions.

White Eagle Over Wimbledon

One of Beirut's most daring correspondents bordering on insanity when the macho competition between reporters to get stories was intense, Juan Carlos used to dress like a Hezbollah soldier with a combat jacket and a long black beard.

The disguise was sometimes if anything too convincing. I once saw him drink three bottles of champagne in the Commodore bar as he recovered from talking his way out from being shot as a suspected Communist militiaman by a Sunni fundamentalist gunman during fierce fighting around the northern city of Tripoli.

'JC' lived in an apartment on the Beirut Corniche below Robert Fisk, another war correspondent, who was then working for The Times.

One day Fisk's Iranian girlfriend Sheherezade threw a surprise birthday party for him, a boozy affair starting in Juan Carlos's flat with caviar that JC brought back from Iran. After a few glasses of champagne, JC and Fisk began singing.

During the festivities, which had moved to Fisk's third floor flat, a fire fight started between militiamen in a shore battery near the house and an Israeli gunboat patrolling the coast. As the machine gun and cannon fire rattled around the palm trees, Fisk reeled onto his balcony.

"These are my men," he ejaculated, gesturing down at the Lebanese fighters, "they've put this on for my birthday."

In a restaurant frequented by fighters, I annoyed an enormous, angry pistol-wielding militiaman who looked as if he was itching to shoot a drunk British reporter He was convinced to spare me retribution on the unlikely ground that he and my father were both good partisans.

The incident caused some mirth in the UPI newsroom on Hamra street the next day. This was the heyday of Islamic militias' kidnappings of Westerners in Beirut.

I have a hazy recollection of being there with Richard Beeston and one of his sisters. Peter "Bill" Smerdon, the brave UPI bureau chief, told me about it the next day.

Walking to and from the office from my apartment next to the Commodore in 1985, I felt some empathy with Dad's hunted condition escaping Poland. Veterans in the office and our charming Lebanese staff such as Diana Saad insisted nobody would be kidnapped who was not a spy.

Smerdon walked regularly to work from his flat on the Green Line battlefront dividing the city each day.

I followed his example gingerly, once almost jumping out of my skin as I wandered through an open fruit and vegetable market near the Commodore to see a carload of grinning, bearded militiamen observe me with piratical glee. With an effort I continued haggling for apples.

I guessed they knew who I was, probably through Ghazi, UPI's bearded driver and bodyguard, but decided to leave me be with nothing more than a teasing fright.

White Eagle Over Wimbledon

Fortunately it was well known that UPI had gone bankrupt and was unable to pay much of a ransom. Anyone who walked through the streets alone usually elicited sympathy in contrast to the hostility engendered by the highly-paid television correspondents who rarely ventured from their hotels without a posse of bodyguards.

Ghazi reputedly run away whenever serious trouble threatened but his brother was a member of Hezbollah, the Iranian-backed militia kidnapping foreigners.

The phone rang in the office in my first week there. Smerdon answered.

"All British journalists out of Beirut within 24 hours," the caller announced. Peter went back to writing up his night lead.

The caller from the self-styled Islamic Jihad, a telephone organisation that served as cover for Iranian intelligence and its proxy Hezbollah, rang to give us the message to our office periodically. We took little notice.

David Myers, the British Ambassador, another Univ. man, looked unruffled, driving around west Beirut in a Jaguar sports car flying the Union Jack on its bonnet without escort.

"Look there's your ambassador going to visit his girlfriend," Ghazi told me as we drove through Hamra in the office Alfa Romeo Giulia. It had tinted windows. Ghazi's occasional claim the Alfa was a "bad car" used for kidnappings seemed plausible.

John McCarthy, the WTN journalist, lived in the apartment next to me. He said a lengthy goodbye to me and everyone else he had met at the Commodore before he was snatched on the airport road. I was always careful to tell nobody except Ghazi of my travel plans when getting out of Beirut. John spent four years in captivity.

Smerdon was abducted in front of the British Embassy at the start of the TWA hijacking in 1985 as he was buying a packet of cigarettes. He was released after a hairy 24 hours spent sprawled in the trunks of threatening Shiite gunmen's cars.

They searched him meticulously in an underground garage and threatened he would be killed "if we find one thing that proves you are a spy."

At the end of the 24 hours he was taken to a stretch of wasteland near the Chatila Palestinian refugee camp and told to walk, fully expecting to receive a bullet in his back.

A few minutes later he hailed a yellow service taxi and told the driver what had happened. "I think they might have been Hezbollah," Smerd said.

"No they weren't," the cab driver said, "because I am."

I flew back into Beirut two days later to help cover the hijacking. Peter was calmly running the office from the news editor's "slot" by the big window looking over the shelled out wasteland behind the office building.

White Eagle Over Wimbledon

"Phillips, welcome back," he said, fixing me with his amused, friendly look that confirmed the bureau under his cool direction was enjoying a high adventure.

Richard Beeston, then of Newsweek, later Foreign Editor of The Times, also nearly got himself killed in Lebanon several times, once talking himself out being shot by Socialist Party PSP militiamen at a checkpoint by simply refusing to lie on the ground as an American colleague, Michael Dawahare, begged on his knees for his life to be spared.

The gunmen stopped Richard's car on the road from Sidon to Beirut. They accused him of spying and lead him and Dawahare into a room with walls splattered with blood.

"What do you mean? I am not lying on the ground, no," Beeston told the gunmen's chief. Eventually in this battle of wills the two were let go. The chief sensed Rick was someone important.

Later when he became renowned Richard rarely spoke of his adventures in Beirut but those who had the privilege to work with him remember them vividly.

These two young Englishmen, Richard and Bill, were unlike anyone I had met in Wimbledon, Oxford or Rome. Their profound belief in courage and dedication to their Lebanese staff and the Lebanese people shook up my ideas and made me realise how soft and corrupt I had become.

Peter I saw again in Cyprus, Africa and Rome. I would run into Richard in a variety of hotspots as well as socially in

London. He went on to be a colleague and then my boss at the Times. His outstanding character was always an inspiration.

During the TWA hijacking, Juan Carlos and I staked out a school where the American passengers from the airplane were being held hostage guarded by Amal gunmen.

Juan Carlos joshed with a group of teenage Amal killers sitting on a jeep carrying a huge recoilless rifle. One boy swivelled the barrel toward JC's chest, a sick joke he acknowledged with a chortle.

I watched as one of the Shiite militiamen yanked a grenade from his satchel, pretended to pull the pin and lobbed it gently toward us reporters. Juan Carlos and I looked at each other in disbelief then sprinted away like maniacs. The Amal thugs' laughter and absence of an explosion stopped us.

This was an old joke that Robert Graves told from France:

"One of our company commanders here is Captain Furber, whose nerves are in pieces. Somebody played a dirty trick on him the other day – rolling a bomb, undetonated, of course, down the cellar steps to frighten him. This was thought a wonderful joke." [57]

The next morning I was ordered away from the school at gunpoint by the Amal press spokesman Ali Hamden as the drama entered its final stages prior to the hostages' release.

White Eagle Over Wimbledon

The UPI Beirut bureau won an Overseas Press Club prize for our coverage of the hijacking.

As a reporter from Rome I spent several days in Lebanon covering visits by Cardinal Etchegerray, a Vatican envoy, who came to give courage to the embattled Christian enclave of Jenin.

To reach Jenin I had to take a taxi through the Druze-controlled Chouf and then across an eery strip of no-man's land in a sunken road to territory controlled by the Christian Lebanese Forces.

One time we stopped to buy two singing birds that a peasant boy was selling by the high grass bank of the road in no-man's land. The Lebanon Taxi driver persuaded me to buy him the birds "for luck" and we drove into Maronite territory.

In the Jenin Church where the Cardinal celebrated mass I found Juan Carlos exciting some curiosity among the tough LF militiamen. "Where did you say you came from Juan Carlos?"

JC blew his brains out with a shotgun, in Cocebamba in 2002 after losing battles against alcohol, cocaine and the unfeeling editors from the Madrid daily *El Pais*.

UPI was the poorest foreign news organisation but we employed the most beautiful and bright young Lebanese women journalists like Diana Saad, who worked later with Agence France Presse in Hong Kong before moving to Australia.

Samia Nakhoul, a beautiful Christian Palestinian, romantically linked to Beeston, went on from the UP to become a Reuters star and was badly wounded by American tank fire in Baghdad.

"I was just thinking," Samia said, sprawled on the sofa in the Newsweek office next to UPI, "if you are kidnapped there is nothing anyone could do for you, nobody could save you."

"I would save you, Samia," Richard said.

As I was accompanying one of the Lebanese office lovelies home one night after dancing at the seaside Summerland Hotel disco into the early hours a shot rang out, ricocheting off the walls of nearby buildings.

"That bloody sniper," the girl cursed. We rushed into the welcome cover of her apartment block and hid in bed.

There was no hiding anything from the alert, friendly porters at the Commodore Hotel, when I arrived back next day, however.

"Where have you been? Was that your second wife?"

David Blundy, a Sunday Times reporter, was another congenial acquaintance in the Back Street, a Beirut night club. Journalists would wind up militiamen drinking there by ordering a 'Jumblatt and Berri,' meaning a J and B whiskey while irreverently toasting Walid Jumblatt and Nabih Berri, the leaders of the Shiite Amal and Druze PSP militias.

White Eagle Over Wimbledon

Blundy was shot and killed in El Salvador a few years later. His daughter Anne went to Univ. at Oxford. She penned The Bad News Bible, a spoof on war journalism in which a foreign editor is exposed as a paedophile.

"Hard-drinking, fast-talking war correspondent Faith Zanetti is on assignment in the Middle East and she loves it - not least because it allows her to avoid her ex-lover, her editor and her past. Even amidst the horrors of present-day Jerusalem, Faith's tough, unsentimental approach gets her leads and scoops the other hacks can only dream of." [58]

Journalists only receive real recognition from colleagues if they are killed, she noted poignantly.

Her father's death was not entirely surprising given his fascination with war. Others like Mick Deane, the jovial husband of Daniela Iacono, were cautious but their luck trickled away because they kept going out.

Egyptian soldiers shot and killed Mick in Cairo while he was filming for Sky in 2013. He was 61.

Many war reporters fantasize about having a private army, as Fisk's birthday party showed.

The romantic notion became reality for Rick Beeston when he was was given honorary command of a company of Druze militiamen by its commanding officer was visiting his home in the Chouf mountains.

When thugs on the fringes of the Shiite Amal militia tried to evict a neighbour of Samya's from her apartment

Richard sent a PSP platoon to the rescue and then deployed his men on other "peace-keeping" missions around the city.

"It was great throwing them into action against the bad guys," he told me.

A natural leader, Richard was able to put into practise in this unorthodox way some of what he learned during a brief spell with the Royal Greenjackets before deciding that he didn't want to make a career with the Army involving long spells in northern Ireland.

His adventures recalled scenes from James Buchan's novel, A Parish of Rich Women, in which a British journalist throws his lot in with the PLO during the Israeli siege of Beirut in 1982.

Buchan described a city "dying of apathy, dying of people sitting all day on their balconies and staring out to sea, dying of rats and wild dogs and rubbish that nobody bothers to burn any more, dying of despair shot through with panic." [59]

Known for his wicked sense of humour, Richard found scope for it when he was trapped in the Commodore Hotel by heavy fighting together with Anglican envoy Terry Waite during one of the mediator's trips to try and free Western hostages.

"Mr Waite, we've decided that since you are the biggest man here we are going to cut you up and eat you," Richard told the emissary, enjoying the look of confusion on the

White Eagle Over Wimbledon

burley clergyman's face before he realised he was having his leg pulled.

The risk of kidnapping was a frequent anxiety while working in the Lebanese civil war.

It was always reassuring to come across Rick strolling nonchalantly around Hamra between militia checkpoints, a tall blonde Englishman conspicuous in the mean streets.

After Beirut I went to open UPI's bureau in Bahrain, in the Persian Gulf, covering the war between Iran and Iraq. From my base in the island emirate I travelled to Kuwait, Dubai, the UAE, Sharjah and Iraq.

Bahrain was an appallingly boring place to live. There was little to do except drink and swim on the "Sheikh's beach," a miniature resort reserved for foreigners so as not to excite the sensibilities of the Shiite majority.

The boredom was relieved when I returned to Rome in July and married my fiancée, Maristella, a beautiful and enchanting ballet dancer at the Teatro dell'Opera. The service was held at her family's parish church in Parioli.

"How was the wine John?" Charlie Ridley asked me on the steps of the Church.

"Catholic weddings are usually grim but I enjoyed that one. What an impressive father-in-law you have. He'll be paying for you from now on, I expect."

The reception was at the Casino Valadier restaurant in the Villa Borghese. The wine we drank was Valpolicella.

We spent our honeymoon in St Tropez and the French Riviera, flying from Rome to Nice and renting a car to drive down to St. Maria de la Mer in the Camargue. The Italian Lira had just undergone one of its periodic devaluations. Paid in dollars, I could then live like a pasha.

Back in Bahrain driving back to my flat in my jeep after a good dinner I overtook a police car. I was stopped and slung into jail in the desert on a trumped-up charge of drunken driving.

After two uncomfortable days in the hot and humid cells with some unusual gentlemen from Saudi Arabia I met a taxi driver I knew who was about to be released. I gave him a note to leave with Julian O'Halloran of the BBC, a friend making a documentary for Newsnight.

Julian put up dlrs 500 to bail me out pending my trial by an Egyptian judge. I was acquitted.

The only way to escape from an assignment that might last three or four years was to get expelled.

Bahrain welcomed news organisations on the unspoken condition they did not report local politics.

After uncovering a plot by Iranian-backed terrorists to blow up the island's oil refinery, a harbinger of the conflict that has divided the island today between the ruling Sunni royal family and the Shia majority, I was duly deported.

The Gulf Daily News published a report headlined "Journalist to leave island."

White Eagle Over Wimbledon

"A British journalist based in Bahrain has been given until the end of the month to leave the island," said the report Jan. 17, 1988.

"John Phillips, aged 32, has been manager of the United Press International Bureau in Bahrain since it was set up last year."

"A Ministry of Information Official said: 'We consider it unwise to continue his sponsorship because he has displayed a lack of judgement."

The report added that "The authorities apparently objected to parts of a report filed by the news agency in Bahrain on a terrorist plot to sabotage the Bapco oil refinery."

"Mr Phillips, who spent four years with UPI in Rome before coming to Bahrain said he was not in a position to comment."

Stella and I moved to a new, more congenial assignment in Paris.

Leon Daniel, my foreign editor at UPI, wrote:

"The foreign correspondents of United Press International often are targets in continuing worldwide assault by governments on press freedom. Unipressers have learned the hard way in recent months that much of the world does not share their view that all people should be free to exchange information, ideas and news."

"John Phillips, now in the Paris bureau, and I were expelled separately from Bahrain, whose government did not approve of the way we were covering the war in the Persian Gulf."

He continued "There is a saying at UPI that if you can't take a joke, you shouldn't have signed on. However if minor harassment by governments goes with a foreign correspondent's territory, UPI views with the utmost seriousness beatings, expulsions and other high crimes against a press that would be free."

In Paris I had the privilege to work with another experienced journalist who became a generous mentor. Philip Jacobson, the Times bureau chief, left me to take over the newspaper's coverage of France when he went to Saudi Arabia to cover the first Gulf War.

I poked gentle fun at the French failure to garner much of the glory in the conflict apart from a dramatic dash by the Foreign Legion. French Air Force pilots were sent gifts of cheese by admirers at home but complained that they felt "useless."

As a result, Le Point magazine reported, The French Ambassador summoned Times Editor, Simon Jenkins, to complain at "The Times' repeated denigration of the French war effort."

"Thank you for your 'denigration of the French war effort,'" foreign editor Martin Ivens (now editor of the Sunday Times) wrote to me in a rare letter of thanks that could have come out of Scoop.

White Eagle Over Wimbledon

From France I travelled to Algeria, chronicling the killing of foreigners and massacres of Algerian civilians. This was one place I never expected Poles had been in significant numbers.

I was wrong. The poet Mickiewicz's verse from his messianic *Book of the Polish Nation and of the Polish Pilgrims*, addressed to the emigration which settled abroad after the failure of the 1831 Rising, identified the Polish nation as the collective reincarnation of Christ:

> *"Almighty God! The children of a warrior nation rise their disarmed hands to you from every quarter of the world.*
>
> *They cry to you from the bottom of Siberian mines and the snows of Kamchatka, from the plains of Algeria and the foreign soil of France ..."*
>
> *"By the blood of all our soldiers fallen in the war of faith and liberty, deliver us O Lord!"* [60]

An attractive Algerian woman spy who latched onto me at the hotel provoked a scene recalling not so much the Warsaw Uprising as the Warsaw Ghetto uprising.

In his account of the Jewish fighters' struggle, Kazik, one of the survivors, related how when in Warsaw outside the ghetto he frequently was challenged by curious Polish girls to prove that he was not a Jew. He would begin pulling down his trousers until the lady told him to stop.

If the Algerian spy had seen my father's AK file where his religion is clearly marked as "Rim Catholic" she might have spared me the sight of her lifting up her dress in my hotel room to reveal that she wore no underwear, presumably a bizarre ploy to see if I might be a spy for Mossad.

"You like?" she said, pointing down with one hand between her legs while the other held the dress. Her body was strong and beautifully made and a hot wind boomed against the shutters of the room, mixing with the sound of crackling machine gun fire from the direction of the Casbah.

She hissed "Show me yours." As a guest in Algeria I decided it would be diplomatic to cooperate. I made my excuses. She left.

"It's called 'getting physical,'" a colleague from the New York Times, Roger Cohen, commented with a chortle when we were back in the St. George's bar some years later. "I wonder what she would have said to me."

Not everyone had a lucky escape from the Algerians. Olivier Quemenère, a French friend working for ABC news, was shot and killed in the Casbah in 1993 at the end of an assignment we shared.

Olivier ignored my warning to stay out of the beautiful quarter built during the Ottoman empire. Little had changed there, it seemed, since the war of Independence, described by journalist Alan Williams in his 1965 novel Barbouze.

Like his fictional reporter Neil Ingleby I was uneasy walking through streets where one was inevitably the only European.

> *"The worst moments were always just before entering and leaving the Casbah, with the walk through the narrow alleys, the tall dark walls ... there was always the chance that someone might decide to take a shot at him from one of a thousand black corners. He would return from each trip exhausted, the back of his neck itching with an over-developed instinct for danger, and try to distract himself ..."* [61]

Philip Shehadi, a quiet Lebanese American reporter for Reuter, with whom I had worked in Kuwait, was knifed to death in his Algiers apartment by a young thug in what was described officially as a "crime of passion."

In Kuwait Philip and I had met Joseph Stafford III, the CIA station chief in Kuwait who was one of the Americans who escaped from the US Embassy in Tehran with the help of British and Canadian counterparts. "I don't mind doing his spooking for him so long as he gives me information in return," Philip said as we enjoyed lunch by the pool of the Kuwait Hilton.

A more uncomfortable sojourn in Sarajevo during the siege in 1993 at the height of the Bosnian war took me to a situation with conditions comparable to those of Warsaw during the Rising.

John Phillips

JP on assignment in Sarajevo during siege by Serb forces 1993.

The courage of the hugely outnumbered Bosnian defenders battling the Serb forces surrounding us recalled for me the bravery against overwhelming odds the Home Army exhibited.

White Eagle Over Wimbledon

Just as the Russians stood by and watched the slaughter in Warsaw then, the international community for years did next to nothing as Bosnian Serb snipers and gunners slaughtered Sarajevo's civilians.

Getting out of the city was harder than getting in. Shuttling to the airport in an armoured personnel carrier driven by black Foreign Legion peace-keepers, a French woman TV journalist and I were caught in cross fire between Serb gunners and Bosnian troops firing rocket propelled grenades.

A young Bosnian soldier helped me pull down the APC roof hatch cover smartly as we careened through the maelstrom and grenades exploded against our vehicle. The Legionnaires cursed, "putain, putain …"

At last we reached the battered airport where a French photographer shared a decent bottle of wine with me as we sat through a heavy bombardment. Two legionnaires were killed by mortar fire while caught patrolling on the runway.

The UN shuttle flight to Split was cancelled. I drove back to the Holiday Inn along Sniper's Alley at 100 mph in a soft-topped car with a New Zealand photographer who had got a scoop with shots of the dying Foreign Legion men for Paris Match.

A rare connection by satellite phone that night from the Reuter's office to London brought a different rocket from the foreign editor of my daily newspaper imploring me to leave the city.

"No mock heroics please John. Just file whatever you can get and get out." It was useless to explain I had been trying all day to do just that.

There was the same sensation of being abandoned by the world and the great powers expressed in the literature of Warsaw. Many commentators would ask why Europe had learned so little from the Second World War.

"Can you tell me what's the point of this?" the mayor of Sarajevo asked as we drove around the city at night to black market restaurants during lulls in the shelling.

"The world just wants to keep Sarajevo as a huge concentration camp."

Back in London the same question was being asked in Angelo's, a Lebanese Club in Westbourne Grove favoured by journalists and spies where I had a full dinner with Telegraph journalist Lewis Jones, with whom I had studied at Univ. and his brother Nick.

After admonishing the clientele to fight with the Bosnian army and act to save Sarajevo from its plight, my inebriated ramblings attracted the attention of the spies.

One spook addressed me from the adjoining cubicle of the Gents in Mario's cellar.

"Do you know what you're talking about?"

"Well, a little, I was in Sarajevo three months ago."

"Were you? Well, the situation has changed now."

"Who the hell are you?" I asked.

White Eagle Over Wimbledon

"Foreign and Commonwealth Office." The spy flushed his lavatory sharply.

"I think it's time to end this conversation now," he said.

I checked into a nearby hotel with a useful all night bar and then took a taxi to the Times office to lobby for a new contract, collapsing inside the News International bunker.

I was taken to the infirmary on a stretcher by security men and then had a tense alcohol free lunch with the foreign editor, followed by breakfast with him soon after. Nurses in the Times clinic charitably diagnosed me as 'suffering from shell shock' from Sarajevo.

The foreign editor was as good as his word and the paper gave me a hard-earned new contract putting me on salary.

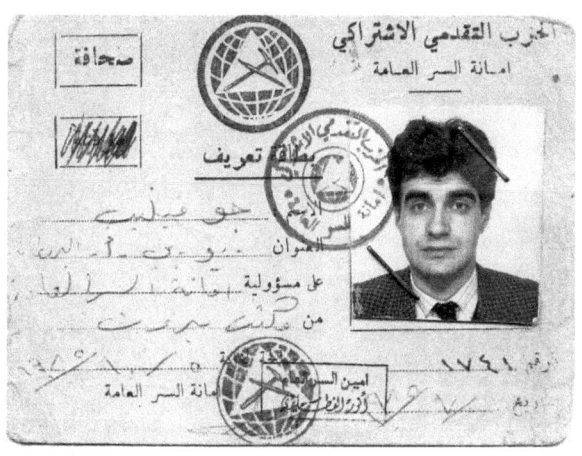

Identity card issued by Druze PSP party, Lebanon, 1985

Chapter 12:
We always go back

"The centre, the dead centre of Europe's centre, Warsaw."
Donald Davie, *A Meeting of Cultures* [62]

I stood on the runway tarmac in bright sunshine in front of the big Sea King helicopter as the Fleet Air Arm pilot warmed up the chopper's powerful Rolls Royce Gnome turboshaft engines. The aviator decided I had sobered up and beckoned me to clamber inside off the runway at the edge of Bari airport. Soon we were scudding agreeably over the waves away from the Apulian coast toward the Royal Navy aircraft carrier, HMS Ark Royal.

On board the carrier I watched as a squadron of Harrier jump jets took off vertically from the carrier, heading to Bosnia to help a British Army patrol escorting an aid convoy that came under attack from Serb forces. Then there was the long copter ride back to Bari with the public relations Lieutenant Commander from Fleet headquarters to send my story.

White Eagle Over Wimbledon

"The trouble with the Poles is that they are always on the winning side," the Lieutenant commander, Andy Withers, told me with a mischievous look on his face over a very liquid lunch at our Bari hotel. This young officer claimed to believe that many Polish officers in the Second world war had collaborated with the Germans as a way of opposing the Russians.

The Senior Service, I discovered, likes to have its own view of history. "It was said in a friendly way and should be taken as such," he retorted with a cheeky grin. The lunch, washed down with several bottles of wine, evidently was designed to vet a reporter before allowing him close to the sensitive Harrier jets.

Unfortunately it also left me tired and emotional when it came to embarking by helicopter for the carrier. At first the Sea King pilot at the Fleet Air Arm facility in Bari airport wouldn't let me on board.

"If there was an emergency I doubt you could react and you could jeopardise the safety of others," he said flatly.

When I did get to the ship after being given 24 hours to sober up for a second attempt at flying, I found myself suffering from mild post traumatic shock syndrome after being shown a disturbing film of Serbia and all but collapsed while trying to interview the Admiral in charge of running the No Fly zone around Bosnia before being medivaced back to Bari.

"Well there that's the last Harrier taking off," the admiral said as I struggled to find a clean page in my notebook. "Are you a defence correspondent?" he asked.

"No sir, I am a Rome correspondent, but I have been to Bosnia and am a bit of a coward," was all I could manage to reply inanely before confessing that I was feeling "rather unwell" and suggesting we postpone the discussion.

As I left the ship I gave a copy of "Farewell my Lovely" by Raymond Chandler to a friendly woman Navy press officer and wrapped a white silk scarf around my neck for the chopper flight back, raising a chortle from Withers. "We'll get you up in a Harrier yet, John," he said.

The ship's doctor, a young officer, sat by me in the crestfallen trip back with the sick journo, occasionally giving me a quizzical thumb's up sign to check his tranquilliser was working.

"What the hell's going on John?" David Watts asked testily as I rang into the Times office in London from Bari airport. "The defence ministry called us to say they had a signal that a journalist had collapsed on the Ark Royal."

Through a mist of champagne, vino and brandies quaffed during the "sobering up" the night before I successfully got the flight out to the Ark on the Sea King, the exciting facility visit evidently had taken on a Hunter Thompsonesque quality of fear and loathing in the Mediterranean.

White Eagle Over Wimbledon

The Foreign desk calmed down, however, when I told them I had a story for the front page about the Harriers going into action over Bosnia for the first time.

"I'll give you a full explanation. I have a story to file."

Withers looked over my shoulder as I somehow pounded out a dispatch. The story had been heading for the front page but fell off the news agenda when the Americans intervened and persuaded the Navy to bring the Harriers back.

It was a sign that I had indulged in too much Algeria and Bosnia, as well as too much Mascara vino. "You're suffering from a mild dose of battle fatigue," Withers said.

Julian O'Halloran summed up the misadventure as I drank the better part of a bottle of whisky in his Brondesbury kitchen weeks later with him and Andrew Lycett. "You counted them all out and then collapsed," he said, referring to a famous BBC dispatch from the Falklands War in which Brian Hanrahan said "I counted them all in and then counted them all back."

It would be another six years before I would see Harriers take off again in anger to pound Serbian targets and enjoy several drinks with the pilots, this time from the light gray RAF rather than the dashing Fleet Air Arm whose Harrier squadrons have long since been disbanded.

Back in the Eternal City a few weeks later however, I learned that my four year spell as Rome correspondent covering the rise of Silvio Berlusconi, the media tycoon, had ended abruptly following a round of vicious office politics in London. I had also undoubtedly made enemies with critical coverage of Berlusconi's bid for power.

One friend was kind enough to compare my sacking to the way the Times had sought to disown its Spanish correspondent George Steer in the 1930s after he broke the story to the world of the Francoist and Nazi bombing of the Basque city of Guernica.

Steer's story appeared on Wednesday, April 28, 1937, on the Times foreign news pages. He identified the aeroplanes in the three and a half hour air raid as German, revealing to the world the "dirty secret that Nazi Germany was deeply embroiled in the Spanish Civil War, hugger mugger with General Franco's 'insurgents,'" wrote Steer's biographer.

"Times correspondents were not named then, so few in England knew who told them about the destruction of the town … Steer's story caused a global outcry." [63]

Rankin also noted that "Steer's messages, however 'useful' had embarrassed The Times. Respectable opinion – and no one could be more respectable than Geoffrey Dawson, Editor of The Times – supported the British government's policy of non-intervention, but at the end of the day would rather have had Franco's side win."

"Steer was valued as a first-rate, bold correspondent, but he was fatally 'viewy', and his views were not Dawson's. The man and the institution parted."

White Eagle Over Wimbledon

My next encounter with the spooks was more civilised than at Angelo's. I met a former army officer called Richard during the interval at the Christmas Pantomime in the English College in Rome. He introduced himself as a political officer specialising in European affairs.

I enjoyed his company and could see he must have been a popular soldier before he joined SIS. Much of his work involved keeping an eye on Libyan activities in Italy lest Col. Gadhafi resume arms supplies to the IRA.

Charles Ridley discouraged such meetings. "Everyone gets approached," he said. "Alright, go off and join SIS then, if you like, if you want to get involved in murdering some poor bastard in a dark alley."

I was living too dangerously already. One evening while working in Kenya I regained consciousness after a long lunch with Angus Campbell, a bibulous friend from Rome, and heard the voice of a man talking what seemed a very long way away. I gradually realised that the voice was mine.

I found myself lying on a mat in a simple shantytown brothel on the outskirts of Nairobi, an area where I was told that white men never went because they were often killed. I may have had a great time with the Masai girls in the establishment but if so I can remember nothing of it.

In summer 1998 I at last travelled to Poland for the first time, fulfilling for the Filipowicz family, I hope, Sim's maxim that "We always go back but maybe not the same ones who go away."

"Why are you crying?" Margaux asked me as we sat in the LOT Polish airlines turbo-prop aircraft rumbling into Warsaw from Prague.

In Warsaw we stayed one night in the comfortable, old world Europejski hotel (since helas closed). A hotel driver who collected us from the airport, a Polish American who had returned after many years in the United States asked us "Do you want to see Auschwitz?"

We boarded the train to Krakow the next day for an emotional re-union with my cousin Andrzej. It was the first time we had seen each other in more than 20 years. "The children," he said, as he met Suzanne and Margaux, "the first children."

As I told him over a beer about all that had happened in the meantime, my father's death, my sister's illness, getting fired by The Times, he said, "John, you deserve a holiday."

Walking through the old city he told me what he knew about the new Underground, Solidarity, and the fortunes of his engineering company that had been privatised since the end of communism.

After a wonderful week in Krakow we went by bus to the mountain resort of Zakopane, which we used as a base for hiking into the Tatra mountains and riding mountain bikes in their foothills. On the road our bus passed by a

White Eagle Over Wimbledon

billboard advertising a brothel on the border with Slovakia, a reminder of how Poland had changed after communism, at least in that frontier area.

Returning to Rome my wife said the trip had explained a lot. "John is not English, he is Polish," she told a friend. Jessie Conrad had a similar impression when she accompanied the great writer to his homeland:

> *"I understood my husband so much better after those months in Poland," Jessie wrote. "So many characteristics that had been strange and unfathomable before, took, as it were their right proportions. I understood that his temperament was that of his countrymen."* [64]

Later in Belgrade I would recall the happy trip to Poland while trying to obtain an interview with General Mladic, the architect of the Srebrenica massacre of some 7,000 Bosnian men and boys, brought comparisons for me, too, with the massacre of Katyn.

Mladic and his cronies in Russian Intelligence may have taken heart from the impunity still enjoyed by the perpetrators of events ordered by Moscow like Katyn.

The Soviet Union admitted responsibility in 1990 for the Katyn massacre but Russia under President Vladmir Putin appears to have returned to denial.

In 2003 the British Foreign Office issued a paper outlining the government's attitude to the killings. "The refusal of successive British governments to charge the USSR with responsibility for Katyn angered many," said Denis MacShane, then Minister for Europe, himself of Polish descent.[65]

While Prime Minister, Tony Blair set up an Anglo-Polish commission to investigate the intelligence contribution made by Poland during the war. Its report highlighted the invaluable work of Polish intelligence officers, often in occupied territory.

"We are tidying up history," a Foreign Office official told the Financial Times. The report is one aspect of intensive efforts to mend outstanding issues between Britain and Poland.

In September 2000 a statue of Gen. Sikorski, designed by Faith Winter, was unveiled in Portland Place, London. The statue "recognises the contribution Sikorski made to sustaining the Polish spirit after the defeat by Germany in 1939."

Ric Todd, the British Ambassador to Poland, in a letter to Rzeczpospolita in 2008 dismissed controversy over Sikorski's death.

"Conspiracy theories that Gen. Sikorski was murdered either by or with the connivance of the British Government, or indeed Winston Churchill personally, are nonsense ..."

"People who travelled by air during the war took risks. General Sikorski was a brave man who took those risks to see his troops and died in a plane crash."

White Eagle Over Wimbledon

Fictional portrayals of Poles fighting in the Second World War also have changed. Patrick Bishop painted an unusually human picture of a Polish fighter pilot in the novel "A Good War," exploring themes of the protagonist Adam Tomaszewski's friendship with an Irish SOE officer.

It probes the darker sides to the Polish Air Force in Britain, notably the tendency of some Polish airmen to shoot German pilots who baled out or to fly over their parachutes causing them to implode.[66]

Cities under siege continued to fascinate me. After Beirut, I travelled to Baghdad and hooked up with Polish engineers working in southern Iraq to take the troop train to Basra under siege by the Ayatollah Khomeini's troops during Saddam Hussein's war with Iran.

Reporting in Tetovo, in Macedonia, in 2001, I got another taste of urban warfare when an ethnic-Albanian suicide bomber and his father were shot dead in front of me at a checkpoint as he tried to throw a grenade into a Macedonian army machine-gun nest.

Many ethnic Albanians felt the two had been unjustly "killed like animals." Peter Nicholls, the Times photographer, who was working with me amid the gunfire, believes we might not have lived to tell the tale if the grenade exploded.

In Belgrade, I met the historian Slobodan G. Markovich whose book British perceptions of Serbia and the Balkans holds true not just for Serbia but for much of the Slavonic world.

Slobodan charted attitudes changing from Orientalism to one where Slav countries were considered warrior states that could be useful, doubtless summing up British thinking on Poland.[67]

In a hangover from the way correspondents used to be treated in Eastern Europe, I was denounced by Tanjug news agency for carrying out a "perfidious interview" with Yugoslav President Kostunica in which he said he would send no more war criminals to the International Tribunal for the former Yugoslavia at the Hague.

Kostunica said his English was so good he didn't need an interpreter but that I misquoted him.

The Tanjug attack was carried by Politika, formerly the official organ of the communist state.

In 2003, I volunteered to go back to Iraq but was left kicking my heels in Rome before being fired over the telephone for the second time as part of yet another budget cut at *The Times*.

On the diplomatic circuit, I met my former Times boss at a dinner for military attachés in Villa Wolkonski.

He had been writing an article about a British agent, Capt. John Armstrong, who was murdered by SS troops in Italy.

The agent's real name was Gabor Adler, a Hungarian who had enlisted in the British army and was recruited by the Special Operations Executive.

White Eagle Over Wimbledon

Reporting the 2001 Macedonian small war.

"Armstrong was a Hungarian Jew," the Times boss said as we gazed at the throng of colourful uniforms. "They all are," he added. He stared with sleepy eyes into the distance.

In 1943 Adler and another agent, an Italian officer who had defected to the British in Africa, were landed by submarine off Sardinia.

They were ordered to organise resistance against the island's fascist Italian garrison. But within 24 hours the pair were captured and sent to Rome, where Adler, 24, was imprisoned until June 3, 1944.

After Gestapo torture, he was executed by the side of the road hours after the Allies entered Rome. A memorial was unveiled at the site of the massacre by the Mayor of Rome.

An honour guard of RAF servicemen and UK defence attaché, Col. Charlie Darell, attended the ceremony.[68]

"He was a Hungarian Jew," my colleague repeated contemptuously as a friend from the Embassy defence section joined us. "Well, he was British when he was shot," she retorted.

Gaby Rado, my classmate from King's College, was only a little luckier than his wartime namesake and countryman who died in Italy.

Gaby was found dead in 2003, in northern Iraq. He had apparently fallen from the roof of the Abu Sanaa Hotel in Sulaimaniyah.[69]

Rado had been reporting for Channel 4 News on the activities of Kurdish fighters and coalition fighters in the area. Channel 4 News said there appeared to be no direct connection between his death and the war.

Although I have sometimes been shot at, however, I have to remind myself that I have not yet been shot in the ear.

Psychologically, however, being sacked brutally from a job to which one gives one's all must be considered similar, involving as it does a deep feeling of rejection.

In some ways the axeing might be said to have been eventually a blessing in disguise. I started litigation against the Times for illegal dismissal and breaking the national journalists' contract.

White Eagle Over Wimbledon

Eventually I received substantial compensation though a further ruling by the Italian judge ordering the newspaper to restore me to my old job as Rome correspondent was ignored.

The legal battle, however, would last five years, during which I would have to provide for my family under difficult circumstances.

I decided I would have to adopt unorthodox methods of guerrilla warfare, in keeping with the Filipowicz spirit of resistance.

The Times office, Belgrade, 2003

Chapter 13:
'Cowards: fire lower'

"The car-hire business is only a temporary sideline with me, of course – I am a journalist by profession ..."
Eric Ambler, *The Light of Day* [70]

"Ecco!" The Italian cashier stamped the English cheque twice on the back and handed over a green 500 euro note and two yellow 50 euro bills.

I felt tense but determined as I walked down the Spanish Steps from the French church of Trinità dei Monti where I sometimes attended Mass, past the house where John Keats died in 1821.

The cashier, Enrico, looked up and smiled as I arrived in his exchange office with the carefully-prepared cheque in my pocket, passing display cabinets packed with boxed sets of Vatican coins bearing the faces of Catholic popes from ages past.

White Eagle Over Wimbledon

"How long do you think the Government will last?" I asked Enrico, an amiable man of about 50 with a pasty, pock-marked face.

"Berlusconi will retire after a year to make way for Montezemolo, the head of Fiat. He wants the job badly," Enrico said.

"That would be a political earthquake."

He studied the cheque before deciding it passed muster. A horse and wooden-wheeled carriage carrying tourists to *Babington's* English tea rooms clattered on the cobbles outside.

Inside the café the lonely lady curator of the Keats-Shelley museum entertained a British military attaché to tea and crumpets. Bright sunshine drenched the tall palm trees reaching for the sky in the piazza and poured into the long room, slicing through the cigarette smoke.

I said an Ave Maria like a mantra during tense seconds that seemed like an eternity.

A cheque takes time to clear Italy's cumbersome banking system. The money would pay for my talented daughter's aeroplane fare for an Oxford University interview.

As the cogs of Italian justice creaked forward in my legal case against News International, I knew that I could count on help from Italian friends, well-versed in the art of *arrangiarsi,* of arranging things or getting by. I was tired of being bullied.

One Times friend, a charming Irishman who also fell from the grace of our masters, found it unbearable to be cast on the scrapheap.

Bill Frost was found dead in his London apartment at age 50 after also losing a battle against cocaine and crack. I last saw him on his way to Bosnia. His Sarajevo dispatches were outstanding. Skill at the top of the reporter's game provided no immunity from addiction or from office politics.

Bill's tragedy convinced me it was a lesser evil to dabble in the Roman underworld than to drink myself to death as Bonnie Prince Charlie, another half Pole (on his mother's side), did in Rome.

I felt a sinister pressure, similar to my father's experience after he was given early retirement from Unilever. Bill's demise showed where one could end if the forces of darkness break you.

My savings soon were spent. I wrote two books about the Near East for Yale University Press. School fees swallowed up the publisher's advances.

Frost's treatment was in the tradition of George Steer, who broke the truth about Guernica for the Times but was practically disowned by the paper.

"Steer was valued as a first-rate, bold correspondent, but he was fatally 'viewy' ... the man and the institution parted."[71]

White Eagle Over Wimbledon

The Times had no official axe to grind on Italy but ultimately rooted for Berlusconi, a personal friend of Murdoch. My dispatches, critical of the media mogul, evidently embarrassed the paper.

The previous prime minister, Lamberto Dini, personally telephoned British Ambassador, Sir Patrick Fairweather, to complain about a story I signed reporting that Dini, nicknamed 'Il Rospo,' (The Toad), was reneging on promises he made to Britain.

Now, instead of the fun of needling prime ministers and being well paid for the sport, it had come down to passing dodgy cheques to survive.

My daughter Suzanne compared our family's precarious situation in those days to Orwell's *Down and Out in Paris and London*. I felt instead rather too much like a character out of *The Light of Day*, by Eric Ambler, perhaps the funniest book ever.

In Ambler's plot, anti-hero Arthur, a self-styled journalist and pornographer, took up stealing travellers' cheques from tourists he ambushed at Athens airport.

As a student I had spent days languishing in the sordid *Murate* prison in Florence after a high-spirited evening in the Tuscan capital went wrong. I did not relish a longer spell inside.

Forty eight hours spent subsequently in a prison in the desert in the Persian Gulf, as local Arab authorities prepared to expel me for my coverage of the Iran-Iraq war, confirmed my dislike of captivity.

I put the money Enrico gave me in my battered wallet and walked out, brisk but not too hurried. I avoided the popes' faces on the coins in his window. The old pontiffs were sure to disapprove.

Turning into the sun-drenched square, I marched down the first side street before going back into the piazza from a far entrance. Skirting the Spanish Steps by the American Express office, I collected my rented car in front of the restaurant La Rampa.

Its tables were packed with beautiful people eating gargantuan plates of pasta. The restaurant soon would be closed as the Finance Police identified the owners as hoodlums from the Calabrian mafia.

I looked around. Nobody followed. Enrico had no inkling that my mother's bank account was long closed.

I brought my mother with me to Rome from England in 2000, effectively abducting her from a dire old people's home in London that recalled accounts of the Bedlam lunatic asylum in 18th century Britain, so that she could live near me.

The warm climate of Italy had worked wonders on her health and through the Church of St Stanislao we had found a young Polish carer, the sister of a nun, who looked after her with great devotion.

White Eagle Over Wimbledon

But now, in hospital on the outskirts of Rome with dementia, she could not have written a cheque for the life of her.

The back of my shirt was drenched with sweat. This caper seemed more stressful than driving down Sniper's Alley in Sarajevo.

At least I found a steady stream of literature on Polish themes to distract me.

In *The Polish Officer*,[72] novelist Alan Furst crafted an engaging portrait of a career intelligence officer's involvement in establishing the ZWZ, Zwiazek Walki Zbrojnej, the Union for Armed Struggle, forerunner of the Home Army.

Some fine action scenes erupt when the hero, Alexander de Milja, leads soldiers escorting a train carrying Polish gold reserves to the Rumanian border to be smuggled to France.

An account of a Resistance reprisal killing of an informer in Warsaw is well researched. Nevertheless, it seems that Furst, like Harris, could not resist implying that all Poles are cracked by pairing de Milja with a deranged wife to whom he makes conjugal visits in a mental home.

More disturbing still to read was *Exodus*, a best seller by Leon Uris,[73] the son of a poor Polish Jewish immigrant to the United States.

This novel sold in more than 20 million copies, billed by Corgi as "the story of an American nurse and an Israeli freedom fighter caught up in the most dramatic event of the 20th century," is highly hostile to Poland both before and after World War 2 and includes a deeply unhistoric account of the Warsaw Ghetto Uprising, claiming that the Home Army refused any help to the Jewish insurgents whatsoever.

For instance he writes: "While the Germans wailed the ZOB tightened their defensive setups and desperately continued to plead for help from the Polish underground. They expanded their plea to the general public, but no arms came, no underground help came, and only a few dozen volunteers crossed into the ghetto 'under the wall' to fight."

Uris conceded that "Poland's own history was blood marked. The Poles had struggled for freedom in a series of wars, revolutions and plays of power "and that in 1939" Poland was a republic ... there were over three million Jews in the country and they formed a vital part of the national life."

But he claimed that "the oppression had not stopped with the formation of a republic. It only varied in degree. There was still unequal taxation for the Jews. There was still economic strangulation. The Jews continued to be blamed by most Poles for causing floods when it rained and drought when it was dry."

Since 1936 there were pogroms, he said, and anti-Jewish rioting in Brzesc, Czestochowa, Przytyk, Minsk Mazowiecki. Uris spoke of "the snarl of hoodlums who specialised in smashing Jewish shops and cutting Jewish beards." After seven centuries in Poland, a Jew "was still an intruder and he knew it."

White Eagle Over Wimbledon

The anti-Polish writing of American writers of Polish Jewish origin such as Uris and Singer is a vast subject in itself.

An exhibit mounted in Poland in March 2014 about the Polish "righteous" who are recognised now by Israel to have saved the lives of tens of thousands of Polish Jews during the Holocaust went some way to redressing the impression given by writers such as Uris.

Their writing has been dubbed Polonophobia and extensive research has been done to set the record straight, for instance refuting and putting in context claims that AK soldiers killed Jews during the Warsaw Uprising.

Nevertheless the country's image was rocked in 2014 when a historian produced research claiming that more Jews were denounced to the Germans by Poles in the Second World War than Germans killed by Poles in Poland. His research does not take into account casualties inflicted by Polish forces fighting outside Poland at Monte Cassino and other battles but still Poland has not yet come to terms with his shocking findings.

A more cheerful discovery in my researches was an account of the historic links between Italy and Poland written by an Italian general.[74]

The two countries' aspirations and struggle for independence had been linked since 1797 when a Polish Legion was set up in Milan made up of Polish exiles who had gone to France after the failed Polish uprising of 1793 led by Tadeusz Kosciuzko.

The Legion was led by Henryk Dabrowski against Austria. It grew to 6,500 men, taking part in the siege of Mantua.

The Legion was accompanied by the so-called Dabrowski mazurka composed in Reggio Emilia by Josef Wybicki, entitled "Poland is not dead," which became the Polish national anthem, including the words "Forward, march, Dabrowski from Italian land to Poland …"

Italians from Mazzini's Young Italy movement fought in the Polish insurrection of 1848 while 250 Poles fought with the Roman Republic from May 16, 1849, at Villa Pamphili, the Villa Corsini and the Porta del Popolo.

Two Polish officers who gave their lives, Captains Podulak and Wern, are recorded with a monument on the via Flaminia and a lane named after Wern in the Villa Sciarra park.

During Garibaldis' defence of Rome, G.M. Trevelyan wrote, "the Poles, too, conspicuous for their long moustaches and their national cap, with its four-cornered crown of red cloth, were foremost in seeking death."

"Homeless sons of the slain mother, they generously offered their blood on behalf of any nation that was at war with tyranny, whether on the Hungarian plain or before the walls of Rome."

White Eagle Over Wimbledon

Wern excited admiration with his careless courage, exposing himself to fire and admonishing the French to fire on his Legion of Honour he had won with the Foreign Legion in Africa.

"Cowards, fire lower," he shouted after he was wounded in the head. The decoration was bathed in his blood. He was pulled down and taken to hospital.

Other Poles fought with Garibaldi in Italy in 1860, notably Gen. Alessandro Izensmid-Milbitz who commanded a brigade at the battle of Volturno.

In 1863 Col. Francesco Nullo, an officer of Garibaldi's who distinguished himself in the conquest of Sicily, led 63 Italian volunteers, most from Bergamo, to help the Poles in the insurrection that year.

Nullo was given command of 500 Poles, 70 French and 62 Italians who fought the Russians against overwhelming odds at Krzykawa near Olkusz, north west of Cracow.

Nullo died heroically together with Elia Marchetti. Another Italian volunteer, Elbano Stanislao Becchi, was taken prisoner by the Russians and shot.

Mussolini's foreign minister, Count Ciano, inaugurated a monument to Nullo in Warsaw in 1939.

Chapter 14: 'Working for the Secret Service'

"He could, of course, wire home to a paper for money; but they would probably refuse him." Eric Ambler, *Uncommon Danger*[75]

I nudged the Fiat Punto through a crowd of tourists buying ice cream near the sprawling gardens of the Villa Medici, the French Academy, planning to drive Suzanne to the airport later to put her on the British Airways flight to England.

A short time later, working in the Vatican on the health of the Pope, I received a call on my mobile telephone from a woman police officer with a gravelly voice." *E lei il Signor Phillips?"*

Would I come to explain why I had kept my rental car for months without paying?

At the entrance to police headquarters in the Piazza Collegio Romano I showed my journalist ID.

White Eagle Over Wimbledon

The inspector, Dr Alfano, was a short, plump man wearing a good quality lightweight grey suit, stripy red shirt and an elegant blue silk tie. He looked at me appraisingly from behind a neat desk as sun poured into the office from a window overlooking an interior garden of palm trees and hybiscum.

"Mr Phillips – Now, what's all this nonsense about these imbeciles at the rent car company wasting valuable police time?"

I gave him a business card. "Ah, *The Times*." The inspector sighed, beaming at me appreciatively. All thought of my having stolen a car was banished by the pleasure of meeting a foreigner representing a hallowed British institution.

"Well then, Mr Phillips," the inspector continued, lowering his voice and pursing his lips as he darted a quick look in my eyes, "so you work for the British Secret Service."

It was more of a statement of fact than a question. "I am afraid not Inspector. I am just a humble peddler of words."

"Come on, Signor Phillips, you can be frank with me. I have known many people from your service, MI6, many of them friends, some even enemies." I insisted I was just a reporter and wondered why he thought otherwise.

I had, it was true, met a suave young agent from SISDE, the Italian counter-intelligence agency, at an MI6 cocktail party in the Villa Wolkonski, the British Ambassador's residence.

I ran into him again once at the Vatican a year or two later, winking at me conspiratorially the day after the head of the Swiss Guards, Alois Estermann, and his wife, Gladys, were murdered May 4, 1998, by one of the young mercenaries protecting Pope John Paul II, Cedric Tornay. Perhaps he had filed an imaginative report about me.

The inspector interrupted my thoughts. "Just please sign this statement. You are going to give the car back to the rental agency in a few days, it says, when you have completed some necessary repairs."

"Do you have a good lawyer? No? Don't worry. I will find one for you."

I had feared I might be cautioned and thrown unceremoniously into one of the station's Fascist era cells. Would a favour be asked in return? The banter over espionage made me uneasy.

"I should like to give you my wife's business card," the good inspector said, handing it to me in both hands, as the interview came to a close.

"My wife, Floriana, is a first class accountant. If you know anyone in the British Secret Service who needs an accountant please give them her contact details."

He got up from his desk and squeezed my hand. "Just let me know please when you have given the car back."

White Eagle Over Wimbledon

I had some anxious moments at police checkpoints after the car's insurance policy expired.

If I had been stopped and found to be driving a vehicle listed as stolen, without insurance, the vehicle would have been impounded. I might be asked why I was driving with a Yugoslav licence.

I worked out where the checkpoints were thrown up each night by police patrols near my flat in Trastevere, steering well clear. The Punto eventually was towed away when I parked it awkwardly near the Vatican.

It seemed a long time since I had arrived in Rome 15 years earlier to begin a dream job with my wife Maristella and our young family.

For a decade I had travelled the Mediterranean, covering small wars in the Balkans and north Africa to test my courage and ensure I wasn't going soft from too much *dolce vita* enjoyment in Rome. Intermittent work as a war and crime reporter could be exhausting and sometimes frightening as well as exhilarating and satisfying.

But Rome was always there to welcome and coax me back to health together with our children, the food, the wine, the weather and the nearby seaside with its sandy beaches and coves.

I had met my wife, a beautiful ballet dancer at Rome's Teatro dell'Opera, while working as a freelancer covering Red Brigades terrorism in Rome in the 1980s.

She had attended Rome's prestigious Tasso lycée with a friend I met in Morocco while hitch hiking around North Africa as a student, Francesco Ghio. The attraction of Africa led me back to Rome.

Francesco and his father showered hospitality on me at their elegant apartment on the Via delle Tre Madonne in Parioli when I was a student in Florence and on holiday from working as a writer at the BBC in London.

Francesco and his friends were all Communists and introduced me to many scions of leading Communist figures. Accused of being 'champagne communists' by detractors, it is true that the Ghios lived well and I was surprised to be served by a maid when invited to his family home on the viale Bruno Bozzi with his parents.

However they also were ready to defend their ideals with their fists. I remember the two Francescos grabbing baseball bats and running out of the studio to rescue local mechanics being attacked by Fascists. Francesco Ghio was a highly civilised man, introducing me to writers such as Cesare Pavese, author of the haunting Resistance novel *Il Compagno*.

This exquisite Roman hospitality was repeated in 1981, when I moved to Rome, by Ghio's friend Francesco Garofalo and his generous father who gave me the use of their family flat in the Corso Trieste for weeks that summer.

I not only fell in love with Stella but became fond of her whole family, running regularly in the Villa Borghese

White Eagle Over Wimbledon

gardens with her brother Alessandro, a young brain surgeon.

"Now John's got all these new relations," Charlie noted approvingly.

We were married in 1987 at her parish church of Saint Teresa in Parioli. The reception was at the Casino Valadier and our honeymoon was on the French Riviera.

I began moonlighting for my daily newspaper in Paris where I was UPI bureau chief. In 1992 the newspaper moved me to Rome to re-open its Italy office.

In quiet periods I would lounge on the beach trying to remember to tune into the BBC World service at the top of each hour. The first summer of my assignment I got a shock when the BBC announced the assassination of the top anti-Mafia judge, Paolo Borsellino. Grabbing my towel I raced to the nearest telephone and then drove like a madman to the airport for the plane to Sicily.

On a sunny morning three years before my summons to the police station, however, everything had changed.

The foreign editor, Martin Fletcher, called me on my cell phone as I was walking to the Foreign Press Club in Humility Street, the via dell'Umiltà, a short time after my first espresso.

"I am going to axe you John," he said. "We have to make cuts in our budget."

"I'll fight this, I'll fight it legally," I spluttered. Fletcher sounded bored.

"Talk to George Brock if you like," Fletcher said and hung up. Brock was the managing editor, the responsible for money on the newspaper. A pompous man, he was immensely proud of his wife working for the British royal family, a connection that did not prevent him eventually being pushed out of the paper.

Years before, when he was European Editor, George had turned up unexpectedly in Rome, supposedly to follow an Italian parliamentary debate on Europe in the Chamber of Deputies, which we arranged for him to attend.

The equipment at the tiny Times office in the Rome newspaper Il Messaggero's run-down building near the Trevi Fountain included a half broken swivel chair with only three ball feet.

George sat on it, the chair collapsed, his arse was on the floor. I laughed. The incident sealed my fate.

John Greaves, my English solicitor, who had been at Univ., was sure a case could be made that the newspaper had broken the Italian journalists' contract that applied to all journalists working in Italy.

The Italian journalists' union handsomely made available for free to me the services of their top labour lawyer, Mara Parpaglioni, who had a reputation for winning her cases.

The dismissal on the telephone was brutal but predictable. The previous year I visited Russia as guest of

White Eagle Over Wimbledon

the Moscow Times, one of the few English-language papers abroad that makes a profit.

I wanted to pick up some tricks of the trade to use to start a newspaper, in the Balkans or Italy.

Highpoints during the trip included a first class Aeroflot flight, courtesy of an upgrade by the generous Rome station chief of the airline, and a visit to the Polish Embassy's fortified residence, where I met a diplomat friend who had agreed to help me apply for Polish nationality.

The diplomat's wife was half Russian and they had plenty of pleasant insights into Moscow, recalling pleasant times we had spent with Jacek at the Tevere Remo club in Rome.

My Russian visa ran out almost as soon as I arrived and shook off the spy who quizzed me in the airport coffee shop.

This meant I had to take the grubby overnight train to Riga, recalling the escape by Mitrokhin, the KGB archivist who defected to the West, along the same route.

I shared a compartment with a friendly junior French embassy employee and his girlfriend who assured me we were lucky it was a Latvian train and not Russian.

In the Latvian capital I kicked my heels waiting for the Russian Embassy to re-open after the week end and issue a new visa, practising my Russian with some of the ethnic Russian girls in the city working in restaurants with names like KGB.

By the Saturday I had run out of money and was avoiding the eye of the receptionist in my hotel in the familiar routine described by Orwell in Down and Out in Paris and London.

A plaintiff call to the Times foreign desk in London to appeal for cash fell on deaf ears.

"We didn't ask you to go there" was the surly response, recalling the plight of Ambler's reporter Kenton, who finds himself penniless in Nuremberg after losing at poker dice to a Polish reporter from the Havas agency.

Kenton knew it was pointless to ask his paper for help since "his contributions were of necessity spasmodic, and if he preferred running around as a free-lance abroad to a nice steady job doing police-court news in London, that was his own affair."

Wandering the brightly-lit Baltic streets I noticed a brass sign on a door for the local Reuter bureau.

My last change was spent at a telephone call box talking to Douglas Hamilton in Belgrade who looked up the name of the Reuter corr. in Riga and kindly agreed to vouch for me.

Minutes later the Reuter manager, a quiet Dutchman, was bewildered to see a half-starving Times correspondent burst into his office. "You've got to help me," I told him dramatically.

White Eagle Over Wimbledon

My new friend in need gave me a wonderful insight into Latvia and the sensitive articles about Cechenia and the employment of Latvian mercenaries there that the Riga authorities had put heavy pressure on the British news agency to suppress.

After moving into a cheap hotel I took the long coach ride back to Moscow and stayed overnight in the Times apartment overlooking the White House that Richard Beeston had arranged for me to use.

Driving through Moscow to the airport the Sunday Times driver pointed out to me the Lubianka, the headquarters of the former KGB and the NKVD where many Polish Home Army officers had been murdered.

I was glad that I had seen only the outside of the Lubianka, with the safety of a British passport in my pocket, and that Dad had not.

Chapter 15:
Down and Out

Which side will you take? The side of good or the side of evil? Truth or falsehood? Love or hatred?"
Fr. Jerzy Popieluszko[76]

Armed police evicted us at dawn from our flat in the Via Archimede one day after a protracted battle with my landlady, a Roman countess married to a retired ambassador, the aptly named Count Carissimo.

Maristella cried. The owner's lawyer sniggered. He arrived with two locksmiths and three armed policemen and a woman bailiff to seal up our apartment.

"This is the Via Archimede, the most expensive street in Rome," the bailiff said. "You must go."

We were told to pack a suitcase each and leave immediately. Unlike Britain or other western European countries, where the state may pay your rent initially if you suddenly lose your job, there is no social security or unemployment benefit in Italy.

White Eagle Over Wimbledon

For three months of an unusually cold winter our family of four lived in a dark one room artist's studio behind the Piazza Navona rented from a radical Irish woman painter, Michelle Rogers.

The place reeked of varnish. Propped against a wall was a huge canvas in oil entitled 'Lampedusa' depicting African immigrants huddled in a boat sailing to Italy. Their plight seemed a comment on our situation.

There was, however, something exhilarating about living right in the centre of the city, even in straitened circumstances.

In the early morning, before the tourists arrived, we had the Bernini fountains in Piazza Navona to ourselves. In the evening it was two minutes' walk to Baffetto's, a pizzeria where the elderly owner encouraged the children to draw portraits of him on paper tablecloths.

We were able to escape at week-ends to a house in the Umbrian countryside near Todi that Beppe rarely used, using a car provided by Fiat thanks also to my generous friend at La Stampa.

In London, Richard Beeston lobbied strenuously on my behalf with the upper echelons of the newspaper, continuing to fight for me in email messages even when he was on assignment in Baghdad.

The genial British Ambassador to Italy, Sir Ivor Roberts, wrote a letter of protest at my treatment to the editor of *The Times*.

Despite such support, Brock poured scorn on my request for a pay-off. "No severance is due and none will be paid," he e-mailed me inaccurately. Steve Turner advised me to keep the email and send it to him after I won the case.

For three more months we lived in two rooms, a step up from the artist's studio, in a flat just behind the Piazza Navona.

Friends rallied round as my English solicitor John Greaves prepared to take the Times to court. In a crowded bar near the Via del Corso Gerry O'Connell, an Irish correspondent, generously lent me money to help pay a deposit for a new flat.

Norman Roberson, a writer at the American Academy who did two tours in Vietnam with the U.S. Marine Corps and seemed indestructible, gave me another wad of cash as he lay on his death bed at a hospice on the Janiculum hill in the last stages of cancer. "I know you'll give it me back," he said days before he expired.

The Death of a Pope

One night in March 2005, as I read while the girls worked on their homework in our cramped flat next to Piazza Navona where we moved from Michelle's studio, the foreign editor of my Washington newspaper, an old UPI friend, called me. Pope John Paul II was on his deathbed.

White Eagle Over Wimbledon

As the agony of the Polish pontiff stretched on until he died April 4, I had a rush of work. I helped smuggle a reporter for *U.S. News and World Report* into the Apostolic palace to view the pontiff's body and sent live television reports from a studio overlooking St. Peter's Basilica as well as writing two or more stories a day for the *Washington Times*.

Regrettably, extreme elements in the Curia, the central Government of the Church, continued to harass a handful of journalists who sought to write the truth about John Paul's final illness.

The Holy See ignored Jacek Palasinski's request to renew his accreditation after he reported in Wprost magazine that the pope's entourage for years delayed treatment for his Parkinson's disease.

During the Conclave we now found a three room apartment in a Fascist area near the Villa Ada park. Several Italian colleagues helped keep me afloat.

Robbing a Bank

I found a tantalising hint of another unorthodox resistance tool in a biography of Georges Simenon, Maigret's creator.

Simenon on his first job in Paris had worked for, Eugène Merle, a newspaper editor who in 1919 launched a satirical review, *Le Merle Blanc*. Simenon termed him a 'blackmailer' whose victims were not individuals but banks.

"He would discover their irregularities and use the information to obtain generous credit ... and he was a specialist in rubber cheques, but he also had a talent for raising new money which he used to pay off his old creditors while bouncing more cheques on his new contributors."

"I sign so many cheques each day that some of them are bound to bounce," Merle told Simenon.

Transferring some money to London through one of my Italian banks allowed me eventually to emulate Merle. For some reason the transfer never arrived.

I protested to the bank's press office. Was this the sort of service one could expect from a leading financial institution?

The manager called me back within minutes. I heard screams of rage in the background as he chastised a clerk for throwing away my transfer request.

The next day he called again. "Mr Phillips, I think we could reconsider that loan you asked for, would you come by my office?"

I had promised Margaux that she could go on the school skiing trip in the Abruzzo mountains. Soon we were kitted out for the ski season.

A full size family apartment near my kids' school became available after I started an English newspaper for the Balkans with my friend Beppe and a sinister henchman of his, Marcello.

White Eagle Over Wimbledon

The newspaper, the *Belgrade Times*, began by suggesting that Serbia restore its royal family to power. "Monarchy – why not?" was the front page headline.

The organ was an idea Richard Beeston and I had conceived independently and was encouraged by Ivor Roberts. It lasted six turbulent months before the Italian managers defenestrated me perfidiously from my own creation.

As the editor I refused to bow to pressure to write articles in favour of the Radical Party, which supported war criminals, nor to kowtow to the Serbian Government.

It was time to move on though for weeks I carried a Sicilian stiletto in my pocket in case I met Marcello.

Chapter 16:
A little sex, no sex

"I've got a restless ancestry behind me. Their ghosts kick."
Eric Linklater, *White-Maa's Saga*[7]

In September 2005 the United Nations Food and Agriculture Organisation, a last resort for journalists on their uppers in Rome, sent me to Asia to report on the agency's work reconstructing the lives of farmers in Thailand, Sri Lanka, the Maldives and Indonesia after the Tsunami that hit south east Asia. This was more like work that I could understand.

In Bangkok as I stepped off the overnight Royal Thai airlines business class flight, I was met on the tarmac by the FAO's media spokesman for south east Asia.

Diderik Develeeschauwer, a resourceful Belgian, had grown up in the Congo when it was a colony of his country. He was wearing shorts and a flowered shirt and smoking a Gauloise.

Diderik whisked me through customs using a special pass and took me to breakfast in a Bangkok coffee shop.

White Eagle Over Wimbledon

"You look tired and bewildered," he said.

"I frequently look like that when I arrive in a new country," I said.

"I'd like to take you to a massage parlour I use. You can have a little sex, a lot of sex or no sex."

I opted for none. As Diderik noted, the young women, paraded in a kind of cage with glass windows, were universally ugly.

"That's where the Director General, Jacques Diouf, likes to stay," he told me as we rode on Bangkok's ultra modern metro railway past a swanky hotel. Diderik was full of useful gossip such as the alleged involvement of the Thai royal family in the illegal drugs trade.

He was the only FAO employee in Bangkok to live in a traditional Thai long house, visiting the girls he had made friends with at the massage parlour in their rural villages when they went home to see their families. "That is how I built up my network."

I soon left westernised Bangkok for Phuket where the tsunami had struck, meeting Thai farmers who had lost relatives and children in the tidal wave.

Virut Hokhua spent 33 years cultivating his fruit orchard but nothing prepared him for the day when dozens of dead and injured people washed up among the trunks of his rambutan and durian fruit trees.

Mr Hokhua, 65, recalled how he helped some of the foreigners carried to his orchard by the tsunami and how a German tourist died there. Among the dead was Mr Hokhua's eldest son, Tamarat, aged 29.

In Aceh province in Indonesia, my next stop, I visited a fish market that the FAO built in the port of Banda Aceh where fishermen could take their catch of tuna and grouper.

Among the sellers chopping tuna was Rizkian Syah, aged 24. He lost all 40 of his family members in the tsunami, including his mother, father and six brothers and sisters.

Until a month before I met him he was living in a tent, eking out a living salvaging and selling scrap iron. His new market job paid the equivalent of dlrs 50 a month.

"In the scrap trade I earned only a little less but it was much heavier work."

With more free time on his hands, Rizkian devoted himself to the sad search that preoccupied so many of the survivors – trying to find his relatives' missing bodies. The stoicism of people in Aceh province was striking.

Aceh province is ruled by a relatively mild form of Shariah law under which gamblers are publicly flogged. I worked there with an Agence France Presse young woman photographer who wore a veil and devoutly prayed as we travelled around the province. Since FAO was running a 'Cash for food' programme in the area I joked to her that Aceh should run a 'lash for food' scheme.

White Eagle Over Wimbledon

My next stop was Sri Lanka where I was entertained by a group of young Italian aid workers staying at a beautiful apartment in Colombo.

The Italian NGO workers had bagged the prettiest girls and the best beaches on the island.

I persuaded the local FAO manager to let me travel to the north of Sri Lanka where we discussed with leaders of the Tamil Tiger guerrilla group a project being implemented almost on auto-pilot, in the sense that the Singhalese and Western staff in Colombo were too scared to travel to the conflict zone.

Unsurprisingly a few years later I wrote about how 1.5 million dollars of FAO funds had been bilked by an employee of the agency in this way through payments to non-existent firms in Tamil-controlled areas.

"Field officers from FAO were aware of the project officer's illicit activities, but stopped short of acting against him because he threatened staffers from the agency would be targeted by contacts he had with the feared Liberation Tigers of Tamil Eelam."

The trip to Asia climaxed with a terrifying visit in a small speedboat through open, high seas to the outlying islands of the Maldives, a fairly unsavoury dictatorship in India's sphere of influence.

Next I returned to my old haunts in Belgrade pursuing a story about the hunt for war criminal Ratko Mladic for the *Independent*.

To pay school fees I borrowed 2000 euros from a Montenegrin loan shark, Black Peter, who helped foreign reporters when Serbia was excluded from the international banking system under UN sanctions.

The shark lent the money illegally, at an interest rate of 10 percent a month. He began threatening strong arm methods to collect and a visit to my home. I appealed to the Serbian Embassy in Rome for help and he backed off.

I was advised not to return to Serbia. In Algeria and Bahrain I had been blacklisted by the governments. In Belgrade I was blacklisted by the Montenegrin underworld. Eventually I did go back to the charming Moskba hotel, looking over my shoulder for a while as I wandered Belgrade in Uncle John's footsteps traced during his 1930 journey from Poland to France.

The Trial

My case against the *Times* was heard in 2006. The Times claimed that it never had a Rome office.

Philip Willan told the judge that there was indeed a Times office with a brass Times plaque on the door in the labrynthine building of the Rome newspaper *Il Messaggero* and that he often saw me working in it.

Dragan Petrovic, the Times' correspondent who worked for me in Belgrade, also appeared in court, after making the journey from Serbia, as a witness on my behalf, together

White Eagle Over Wimbledon

with Valerio Pellizzari, whose office was next to mine in the *Messaggero*.

The Times had three witnesses testifying against me. Richard Owen, my avuncular former foreign editor had sent me to many strange places ranging from Bosnia to Algeria. He confirmed that I had been fired by Fletcher over the telephone – a practise that fitted the macho Murdoch style of management in London but was illegal in Italy where dismissals have to be by registered letter. 'How did you know Mr Phillips was dismissed by telephone?' Judge Grisanti asked.

"I knew because Fletcher called me to tell me he had done it," Richard replied, settling the matter.

David Watts, a foreign desk friend, told the judge he was "not really in a position to judge his work. I am an expert on Asia. John is an expert on Italy and the Balkans."

Asked by the judge if he sat in on my meetings with Fletcher when I returned to London, David explained that Fletcher was jealous of David's relationship with reporters in the field and kept him out of such discussions.

Mr Brock, the newspaper's most important witness, surprised the judge by saying he couldn't recall whether he had seen me at a lunch for European correspondents that Times editor Peter Stothard gave at the Reform Club. I had been sitting next to George at the high table during the gruesome *colazione*.

John Phillips

Hollow Victory?

Three years after we started proceedings against the paper, Judge Eugenio Grisanti ruled that I was an employee of the paper. He ordered the newspaper to pay me 300,000 euros and reinstate me in my old job. The *Times* refused to pay the compensation ordered by the Italian judge.

"We do not recognise the judgement and intend to appeal," the *Times* managing editor wrote.

Since the judge had ruled my original dismissal was illegal and null, the managing editor fired me again, this time in writing. It was the third time I had been sacked by the newspaper and the fourth I was dismissed by News International – surely a record.

The British Association of Journalists (BAJ) in London stepped into the fray, providing me with a brilliant young woman barrister who registered the Italian judgement at the High Court in London, meaning we could send the bailiffs into the *Times* offices to seize assets if they did not pay.

The *Times* obtained a suspension of execution in the High Court on the ground that if they paid me and won in appeal in Italy they would be unable to get the money back.

High Court judge Sir Charles Gray rejected a request by the *Times* barrister for costs of £57,000 to be awarded against me, however.

We would be booted out of another home before the *Times* paid up, but not before my daughter had finished her final "Bac" exams at the French school.

White Eagle Over Wimbledon

Despite the turmoil, Suzanne received the highest mark of her year for science, winning a place at Oxford University – to read biology at Worcester College where Rupert Murdoch studied.

The now familiar drama of police, bailiffs and locksmiths was repeated. The bailiffs' assistants smashed the locks on the door with hammers for half an hour before we negotiated permission to remove our furniture.

An American friend passed us another flat in the chic area of Trastevere. Some of our possessions were stolen in the move but at last we were leaving the Fascist areas of Rome for a more family-friendly district.

My mother died June 14, 2008, in the Roman nursing home where she had lived during the last stages of her illness. We arranged her repatriation to be buried with my father in England after a funeral in the Basilica of St. Silvestro. Diana attended the burial service in west London, carried out by Fr Gula's successor.

Then it was back to business in the Mediterranean. A few months later an editor in Washington called. "John could you shoot over to Libya? Condoleeza Rice is meeting Gadhafi for the first time." I flew to Tripoli.

We watched as Gadhafi greeted Rice in the Tripoli military barracks, marking one of the Colonel's last diplomatic triumphs before the violent popular revolt that overthrew him.

John Phillips

Payback Time

Back in Rome, the appeal court judge accepted our application to get the *Times'* appeal in the case brought forward by six months on ground of urgent need.

On the steps of the court in April 2009 the newspaper's Italian lawyer at last made a serious offer to settle the case. Lawyer Mara Parpaglioni and I decided not to accept it and to see the outcome of the appeal but the case then was adjourned to September to allow negotiation. Steve Turner, President of BAJ, negotiated a final settlement during the summer in a hard-fought victory by the British and Italian unions against News International's bullying style of management.

I went back to the Spanish Steps to Enrico's change office to re-pay him at last for the dud cheques he accepted years earlier.

"Are you looking for your country of origin?" a young German woman had asked me in Sri Lanka at an aid workers' party, eyeing a book I had with me.

Country of Origin, by the Dutch writer E. Du Perron, recounts his life in the former colony of the Dutch East Indies, now Indonesia.

Known as the Proust of the Netherlands, Du Perron wrote a convincing description that I could empathise with about a family becoming ruined and the challenging effect, explored also by Pasternak in *Dr Zhivago*, of going from riches to rags.

Chapter 17:
Return to Lubartow

"It's very provoking, when I'm in Poland people talk about 'You Frenchmen,' and when I'm in France they say 'You Poles!'"
Prince Léon Radziwill[78]

In August 2010, I drove 300 miles from Warsaw to my father's home town of Lubartow near the beautiful city of Lublin with my cousin Andrzej. He had come up to the capital from Krakow in his wife's doughty Twingo car to help me search for my grandparents' grave.

The long trip to Lublin in a Fiat Punto borrowed from Jacek Palasinski, now a popular anchorman in Poland for TVN news, helped cement my friendship with Andrzej, narrowing the gap that existed when we first met as different young men decades earlier.

Enmeshed in suffocating middle class comfort in Wimbledon and uncertain what I wanted to do with my life,

I shamefully had little empathy then with a visitor and relative from Poland.

I knew that we were from the same family but not much more than that and boorishly refrained from finding out more.

Now there was plenty to talk about on the enjoyable drive southeast. The trip was also a baptism of fire into driving in Poland as heavy commercial traffic jostled within the confines of a narrow state highway lined with forests and lush farmland.

Eventually we arrived at Lubartow's Roman Catholic Cemetery, which stretches across land opposite the town's imposing Basilica.

"Do you know where the Filipowicz family tomb is?" Andrzej asked a florist at a kiosque.

The flower salesman certainly did. His own name was Filipowicz. He was evidently a distant cousin. We discovered a number of tombs in the cemetery from different branches of our family.

After we had walked around the graveyard for some time trying to follow the florist's directions, Andrzej shouted that he had found the tomb of my grandmother Genowefa and my grandfather Waclaw.

Half a dozen other relatives lie buried there with them, many of them from my grandmother's Derecki family including one gentleman who lived most of his life in Argentina.

White Eagle Over Wimbledon

Andrzej Filipowicz

It was a peaceful place in front of a large cupressus tree with a life size statue of the Madonna in a blue cloak presiding over the tomb – a fine position in the cemetery.

As if the emotion from finding my grandparents' grave was not enough, there was another surprise. On the top of the main tombstone a smaller headstone had been added recording the death of my father, after he was buried in London.

"In memory of Ireneusz Marek Filipowicz, London, Nov. 5, 1984."

Dad had never been able to visit his parents' grave. I was fortunate to be able to do so and discover that he was still remembered in his home town in the 21st century.

The Cypress tree at the family tomb recalled for me the trees that my father had planted and nurtured in our garden in Belvedere Drive. Our old house there was sold again in 2012 for £2 million. Its façade guarding its 17 rooms had changed little in the last 40 years.

Two of the big trees Dad planted are still growing. The wall we built has been replaced. The layout of the front garden remains the same.

After some time spent in prayer and contemplation in this holy little garden in Lubartow that nobody could take away from us and our family, Andrzej and I visited the sacristy of the Basilica to try and find out who had erected the stone. The priest we met, however, was unable to enlighten us on that point.

Andrzej pored through the parish records and found references to the baptism of Uncle John and other family members written in cyrillic Russian during the era when Lublin was ruled by Czarist Russia before the First World War.

White Eagle Over Wimbledon

It seemed that the stone recalling Dad might well have been put up by cousin Mirek, who had himself died subsequently after a long battle with leukemia. "You see he was not as bad as you thought," Andrzej commented.

Evidently Dad's desertion from the Communist army had long been forgotten by the time of his death. Or perhaps by 1984 graves of former AK men no longer were subject to scrutiny by the authorities who had their hands full dealing with modern rebels.

At the West London cemetery where he is buried Dad is recalled on his headstone as Ireneusz Marek Phillips. In the Lubartow cemetery he is remembered as Ireneusz Marek Filipowicz.

This subtle contrast came to mind when I read an account by an American journalist who worked in Poland immediately after the Second World War.[79]

Paula Fox visited the former estate of an aristocrat in the Tatra mountains. The Polish Government converted it into a "kind of recovery residence for children who had been born in concentration camps or had spent part of their childhood in them. Their parents without exception had been murdered by the Nazis."

She added in her book, *The Coldest Winter*, that "A boy whose name in English would have been Richard asked me to call him that through the interpreter. He didn't want his Polish name; he'd thrown it away."

Had Dad wanted to "throw away" his Polish name when he settled in England? Uncle John, also, had "thrown away" the Polish surname though just to confuse matters he took a slightly different English surname Philip, rather than Phillips.

In Lublin, I discovered, Mirek had become a well-known figure in the local intelligentsia.

In 2008 the local radio station broadcast a special programme to mark the 10th anniversary of his death, recalling his career as the director of an avant garde cabaret show entitled appropriately "Sex" as well as his book on Polish commandos that he researched in London.

His widow Ewa described his courage in his struggle with cancer.

"Poles revere their ancestors," says Ewa Lipmiacka (another Ewa, not Miroslav's wife) in her humorous, perceptive book, the Xenophobe's guide to the Poles.[80]

"Families trek from one end of the country, and even come from other countries, to visit family graves, and they spend hours planning elaborate itineraries to fit everyone in. The glow from the candles in larger cemeteries can be seen for miles."

Cemeteries are almost never empty. "Families tend graves as carefully as they do their front gardens." She notes that "funerals are widely attended and death is, logically enough, the second most popular topic of conversation after health."

White Eagle Over Wimbledon

Andrzej recounted how he had discussed our family roots with a cousin, Anna Filipowicz-Sosnowska, a doctor who worked in the United States and was president of the International Association of Rheumatologists.

While in America Anna had spoken to an expert on genealogy who told her that the Filipowicz family was "probably minor aristocracy" from the Szlachta, the hereditary Polish gentry.

"When she told me this, I just burst out laughing," Andrzej said. "It seemed so irrelevant to my daily life." Three Filipowicz family crests are registered in Polish genealogical records.

Andrzej's healthy reaction recalled for me that of Witold Gombrowicz, who was gripped by the genealogy of his wealthy family as a young boy, drawing up a family tree. He used to tease his avant-garde literary friends with the knowledge in Warsaw before the war.

"I sit down and immediately emphasize, just in passing through, that my grandmother was a cousin of the Spanish Bourbons."

"After saying which I politely pass them the sugar. But not to Casimir (who ruled them because he was the best poet), but to Henry (who had a higher social standing because his father was a colonel). When the discussion begins, however, I take Stefan's side, because he is from a landowning family." [81]

Gombrowicz found himself in Argentina without a penny, having lost his estate, everything material. "I was introduced into the literary world and it was up to me to win these people with intelligent behaviour. Instead I offered them genealogy and made them smile indulgently."

I was not over surprised to read that Mirek had rated Gombrowicz, an anti-nationalist, as one of his foremost influences.

In Lublin, Andrzej and I visited the archives of the Institute for Remembrance, a controversial research body that is custodian of Poland's communist era secret police files.

I filed a request for a search of any record of my father, with the help of a prominent Polish historian, Rafal Wnuk.

Poland decided in 2001 to open the files from the Communist era of the political police, the Sluzba Bezpieczenstwa (SB), which was dissolved in 1990. The Institute for National Memory (IPN) was created in 2000 to manage the SB archives and open the files to interested parties.

The Institute decides whether a person who applies to see his files can be considered a victim of the regime from 1944 or not. In the dossiers made available to citizens the names of informers were cancelled though it was possible to know their identity by making a special request.[82]

The head of Poland's intelligence services in 2001, Janusz Palubicki, formerly a national leader of Solidarnosc

White Eagle Over Wimbledon

emprisoned when martial law was imposed in 1981, was sceptical about the true value of opening up the SB files. "Most of the dossiers of opposition figures likely to play a role in public life were expurgated in 1989," he said.

IPN in Lublin produced no trace of a dossier on Dad. Prof. Wnuk pronounced Dad's odyssey "typical of a Home Army soldier at the time," noting however with a laugh that it had been an achievement "to keep in contact with the anti-communist movement while being in the Communist army."

Dad would have gone on the run after some of his old Home Army contacts were arrested by the NKVD, he added. Possibly he may have been warned by the AK's own agents who had penetrated the new Communist administration.

As Blackwell noted "from the beginning of August (1944) Bureau II of the AK command in the region reoriented its work towards the activities of the Red Army, PKWN, Berling Army and NKVD.

By the autumn, the framework of a counter-intelligence operation had been established by Bureau II. Capt. Antoni Wieczorek, "Scibor," later known as "Kaktus," headed the counter-intelligence unit during August. This unit was able to penetrate the workings of the fledgling administration."[83]

Prof. Wnuk identified Dad's direct commanding officer as Capt. Stefan Debicki, a partisan who used the codenames Jaxa or Jaksa and Kmicic or Kmita. He led the Lublin city

Undergound from April 1944 to Sept. 26, 1944, when he was arrested by the NKVD and sentenced to death.

Jaksa escaped from Lublin Castle on the night of Feb. 18, 1945. Partisans burst into the castle and released him and 10 other AK men being held prisoner, killing two UB guards who resisted.

After the war Jaksa and a group of other WIN anti-communist resistance fighters moved to Gdansk. They thought the port's proximity to Sweden would allow them to maintain easier contacts with the West.

Jaksa eventually settled in the town of Slupsk, in central Pomerania, northern Poland. Under the name of Casimir Linke, he began working as a forester.

He was killed in a firefight with Communist soldiers of the UB in July 1946 after a woman informer denounced him to the secret police.

In 2005 the Institute for Memory in Gdansk war crimes department appealed for surviving witnesses to help bring to justice those responsible for the killing of Jaksa.

A few days earlier I had flown to Gdansk from Warsaw and stayed at the nearby resort of Sopot with my daughter Margaux.

On Sopot's white beach we caught the last rays of Baltic summer sun. The indomitable spirit of Jaksa evidently lives on in the Gdansk area as I discovered when I asked for an ashtray at the bar in our hotel in a converted hunting lodge by the beach.

White Eagle Over Wimbledon

"Of course you can smoke, sir," the young barman told me, "Poland is still a free country."

Margaux and I had more time on this trip to explore Warsaw, celebrated by the modern Yorkshire poet Donald Davie who wrote:

The old town,
Rebuilt, is a clockwork toy.
I walked abroad in it,

Charmed and waylaid
By a nursery joy:
Hansel's and Gretel's city!

Their house of gingerbread
That lately in
Horrific forest glooms of Germany

Bared its ferocity
Anew resumes its gift
For rocking-horse rooms

In Polish rococo

After Andrzej and I left the IPN office in Lublin, we returned to our car, the Fiat Punto which Jacek in Warsaw had lent me. An obvious watcher from some secret service or other was sitting in a parked car directly behind ours on the edge of the Stare Miasto (Old Town).

The old Communist apparatus in the intelligence services had not been swept away entirely in the new Poland. It was still worth keeping an eye on an English reporter asking questions.

Some experts claim that Lublin was the true birthplace of the Solidarity movement that defeated Communism, arguing that a strike in Lublin in May 1980, four months before the Gdansk shipyard sit-ins, decisively demonstrated the power of workers' self-organization in the country.

As we drove away from Lubartow, where we had returned to ask the priest if he had found any more information in the parish records about our family, I realised with a reporter's instinct that we had failed to enquire about the town's darker side.

"We forgot to ask the priest about what happened to the Lubartow Jews," I told Andrzej.

"John," Andrzej said in some exasperation, "do you want to go back to ask about the Jews?"

We didn't but Jacek Palasinski had indicated that the story was terrible, as I discovered when I looked it up on Polish Wikipedia. The first deportation from the town started 9 April 1942.

On the first day, 800 Jews who did not have work cards were ordered to go to the railway station, from which they were taken to Belzec death camp. The last deportation was Oct. 11, 1942.

White Eagle Over Wimbledon

Some deportees were sent to Majdanek, with others going to the death camp in Treblinka. Jews who were found hiding were shot. In total, the number of Jews found after the last deportation numbered 300.

After the last deportations, the synagogues and cemeteries were destroyed. The gravestones were used in a pavement at a Wehrmacht base. At the end of the war only 40 Jews had survived the mass murder, five of whom had stayed in Lubartów.

The town's website understandably balances this tragic chapter of its history with references to some of its happier sons, for instance claiming as a resident Jan Kochanowski, the greatest Polish poet and man of letters in the Renaissance, who died in Lublin of a heart attack in 1584.

In addition to the emotional discovery of the family tomb, the trip inspired me to redouble efforts to find more about the Filipowicz past. Some clues turned into false trails. Reading Blackwell's fine work on the AK in Lublin I was excited to come across this section:

"As part of the same three-pronged attack, a battalion from the 27th Volhynian Division, which was commanded by Captain Filipowicz, was operating around the mouth of the Wieprz River. This area, around the Wieprz River mouth and the River Tysmience, was an area of swampland and marsh."

"This terrain provided good cover for the unit's attack on the town of Kock, which they took successfully along with weapons, vehicles and enemy prisoners." [84]

In its final days of its existence as a fighting force, the 27th Volhynian Division was based in and around Lubartow, raising my hopes of a family connection to the good captain.

Tracing AK records I identified the officer as Lieut. Kazimierz Filipowicz, nom de guerre "Kord," a teacher who was active in the Home Army. He returned to teaching after the war and a period of difficulty with the Communist authorities. However I could find no link in his story to our family.

Despite such setbacks I remain convinced there is much to discover. I was encouraged to read another odyssey by a former student from University College in Oxford, V.S. Naipaul, who spent as long as a year in India researching the roots of a grandfather who had left there for Trinidad.

Naipaul concluded that he was "homeless." His home was neither in India or Trinidad.

My sister Diana and I's link to Poland was perhaps slightly less tenuous, providing the option of "double patriotism" and the curious alliance noted by Robert Kowerski in the Anglo-Polish children between "solid British phlegm and Polish fantasy."

In London later I turned again for advice to Fr. Gula at St John the Evangelist's Church in Putney. He recalled how

White Eagle Over Wimbledon

he had bought it for the Polish community 40 years ago from the Anglican Commissioners who were planning to sell the land to commercial developers.

"People said to me 'there is no point buying a church for the Polish community in London. They are all elderly people and soon they will be dead," my old friend told me as we chatted in a pew.

"On Christmas Eve we had two midnight Mass services with 600 and 400 people attending. Last Sunday there were 1500 worshippers in the Church for Mass."

The work involved in realising his dream took its toll on Fr Gula's health, leading to his suffering a debilitating stroke and more recently diabetes but he had no regrets.

"Christ gave up his health, his life, and we must serve Christ," he said, looking at the beautifully carved scenes from the Stations of the Cross on the walls of the church.

Fr. Gula had the idea for purchasing the church after arranging with an Anglican priest to co-celebrate a wedding in St John's between a Polish girl and a young English man.

"I would like to have such a church," he told his Anglican colleague. "Well, if you like you could buy it," the Church of England priest replied.

He paid 150,000 pounds for the church, (worth at least 1 million pounds today) raising the money through a loan in the United States with the help of Poles all over London.

In respect for its Anglican origins the Poles had retained all memorial tablets in the walls of the Church as well as its original name.

Before he was ordained Fr. Gula had fought in the AK in a unit based in southern Lublin. His unit had set off for Warsaw during the Uprising in response to the request by Bor Komorowski for relief of the AK forces in the capital.

"We were stopped by the Russians who took away our pistols. When I got back to Lublin I was warned by friends not to go home because Russian agents were waiting to arrest me."

My old friend was intrigued to hear about Andrzej and my visit to Lublin and what Prof. Wnuk had told us about the AK there. He had never met Jaksa but knew who he was.

"I was a machine gun loader," he recalled as we ate lunch in a modest café in Putney High street, "it was better to fight than to end your life in a camp."

I arranged to consult the parish records for details of my father's funeral to prove that he was dead as required by the Home Office when I requested to see the Security Service file on him in Kew.

"If you write this book I think it will be very good for you," Fr Gula said. I told him that I often thought of how he told me had acquired his church one day and one brick at a time, never daring to imagine how beautiful it would be at the end.

The meeting was my last with this faithful spiritual advisor and family friend who had guided me as a young man through the trauma of my father's death and in the uncertain years afterwards.

He turned a blind eye when I had turned up late to his sacristy for an appointment, somewhat the worse for wear after a heavy lunch with Charles Ridley at Daquise Polish restaurant. We had been reminiscing, while eating bigos washed down with copious rations of vodka, about Charles' time fighting with the Carpathian soldiers in Monte Cassino.

"Here let me help you write," the old priest said kindly as I struggled to compose a letter to the new parish priest of St. John's asking him to hold a memorial Mass for my father.

A member of the Society of Christ, an order set up specifically to minister to the Polish diaspora, Fr. Gula died Sept. 21, 2012, aged 86, after 35 years of service at St John the Evangelist Polish Church. That followed a spell in Australia as a young priest soon after his time in the Resistance.

He also had acted in the film Inka, about Danuta Siedzikowna, a nurse of the Home Army, who was shot by a Communist executioner in Gdansk jail Aug. 28, 1946.

Fr. Gula played the part of Fr Marian Prusak, who told the world about Inka after giving her the last rites in prison.

The book also often seemed an insurmountable obstacle but it would be finished one day. Many times I was tempted to give up the manuscript as I had several others but I was inspired to persevere when re-reading the encouraging words of Fr Gula in the 1980s when talking about my book work.

"That is your treasure. In this way you can become independent."

At the end of my return trip from Lublin to Warsaw, I dropped Andrzej at his sister-in-law's flat where he was staying and then headed for Jacek's home.

I was exhausted from the long drive along the narrow road packed with lorries. The unfamiliar Warsaw streets lined with anonymous apartment blocks looked all the same as I searched for an elusive turning off a main road.

I found it and spun the wheel. The car shuddered. I thought I must have hit a hidden kerb. Instead a new white Fiat 500 swerved in front of me. A young man jumped out to inspect damage he said I'd inflicted.

"I only borrowed my girlfriend's new car for five minutes to buy cigarettes," he fumed.

"You see that smoking is dangerous," I replied.

There was little evident damage to Jacek's car. Eventually I arranged to pay the youngster a hefty sum, left with Andrzej for the purpose, to cover the repair expenses.

"It seems very strange," I said suspiciously. "Are you sure the damage wasn't there before?"

White Eagle Over Wimbledon

The young man snorted. "You English people always say that things in Poland are strange."

I returned at last to Jacek's elegant home full of plants and cats where he patiently perused once again my father's papers provided by the Polish Underground Trust. "It says no medals," he mused, not for the first time. Andrzej drove me the next day to Warsaw's anonymous airport.

A young nun in a white habit shamelessly jumped to the front of the queue as I waited to check my luggage.

"See you again in Rome or London," I said to Andrzej. "Or in Poland," he replied with a smile.

"That's quite possible."

Suzanne, my daughter, has been doing some reflecting of her own on her background, trying to make sense of having English, Italian and Polish roots. Last Christmas she gave me a present of a book, "Exceptional People. How Migration Shaped Our World and Will Define Our future."[85]

On the flyleaf of the book Suzanne wrote to me that "After all migration has definitely shaped our world to make us an exceptional family."

I prefer to think of my father as a political refugee, a defector and "a deserter from the Polish army who disliked Communism," as he described himself to the British police who interrogated him. It is true that he once described himself to me as arriving in Dover as "a poor Polish immigrant," as a young man, gently admonishing me for frittering away the opportunities I enjoyed at the same age.

The sacrifices he made for his children baffled some people. "Why did he decide to send you to an English public school?" my old tutor from Univ., Leslie Mitchell, mused as we sat in Otello's restaurant on a rainy evening in Rome mulling memories of life 40 years past.

"Why not a grammar school, or even a state school might have been better?"

Perhaps, but I doubt I would have got to Oxford without the benevolent guidance of the likes of Geoff Taylor and Frank Miles.

I concurred with Leslie, however, that Univ.'s admissions process had done well to pluck outsiders like Andrew Tarnowski and myself into a special community where we could benefit from the magic of tutorials, the college library, the JCR cricket match against dons and late nights with coffee and whiskey into the early hours.

The ambiguous historic status of Polish exiles as refugees or migrants and their status in Polish mythology as pilgrims has been examined profoundly by Neil Ascherson in his book about the Black Sea.

In Rome my mates and I started a new English-language newspaper in 2009, *The Italian Insider*. Like many good ideas it had originally developed from Richard Beeston's inspiration and suggestion in 2000 as we sat in the Writer's Club in Belgrade that

White Eagle Over Wimbledon

an English-language newspaper like the *Moscow Times* could be a fruitful and amusingly subversive project to nurture.

I saw Rick last in early 2012 over lunch at St. Catherine's Dock near The Times office. He cast a professional eye over an early copy of the Italian Insider. "Handsome fellow, wasn't he?" he observed as he perused an obituary of Charles Ridley, who had worked with Rick's father in Beirut. "He was in special forces," he noted approvingly.

"Well yes, scouts," I said, imagining Charles dismounting from his armoured car to go to the aid of a wounded NCO in the lead car in a celebrated action. Hundreds of friends of Richard attended a memorial ceremony for him at St. Bride's Church in September 2013. It seemed I was the only one there who had worked with him in Beirut.

A memory came back of walking apprehensively through the streets of Hamra on my way to the office and meeting Rick grinning broadly, totally unruffled – a tall blonde Englishman who stuck out like a sore thumb on the mean streets of Beirut. Kidnapping was always on one's mind then. We had survived what was perhaps our most exciting adventure. Recollections returned of long dinners on the Corniche when Richard and I were the only English reporters left in the 'war-torn city.'

I recalled another time by the River Sava in Belgrade in 2004 with Rick muttering angrily about the behaviour of a drunken English woman from an NGO "letting down our country" by blacking out in front of the *Times'* Serbian staff at the Rejka restaurant, a favourite hangout on the river Sava for young Serbs and foreigners.

I was grateful to Rick for having supported me through so many battles at the *Times*. I wandered through the crowd of mourners at the wine bar near St Bride's where a wake was under way spotting some old faces from former Yugoslavia such as our charming friend with a heart of gold, Janine di Giovanni.

A group of Kurdish politicians recalled Rick's work exposing the genocide of Kurds by Saddam Hussein in Iraq. Even in Beirut Richard had found the Kurds one of the most fascinating of Lebanon's kaleidoscope of ethnic groups, poking fun at their "cruel Kurdish humour."

Several Italian Insider readers, meanwhile, have asked the identity of one of the paper's most prolific and iconoclastic journalists who uses the pseudonym Jan Filipowicz.

The editor opened one the other day. "Mr Filipowicz has got his facts wrong," it said.

Acknowledgements

I am grateful to the following people for their advice and encouragement:

Patrick Bishop, James Blackwell, Gerard O'Connell, Richard Foreman, Maggie Fox, the late Father Jozef Gula, Andrew Hayward, John Heineman, Michael Mewshaw, Dr Leslie Mitchell, James Montgomery, Jacek Palasinski, Anna Dubravska Spake, Dr Bryan Stokes and Ms Gemma Ind of the KCS Old Boys Association. Jonathan Tubbs, Tony Ullman, Peter Walker, Prof. Rafal Wnuk, Adam Zamoyski.

David Petrie, Desmond O'Grady, Andy Hayward, Maciej Gablankowski and Anna Pasieka, Adam Pluszka, Monika Regulska, Megan Williams and Malgorzata Wycz kindly read draft manuscripts and offered helpful and insightful suggestions.

I thank Mr Chris Ransted of the Public Records Office at Kew and Mrs Goddard of the RAF Records Polish Enquiries Section for their assistance.

The biggest debt is to my family in London, Rome and Krakow including Andrzej Filipowicz, Diana, Margaux, Suzanne and Maristella Phillips.

Any errors of fact or recollection are my own.

Notes

[1] Dagmar Rita Myślińska," Post-Brexit hate crimes against Poles are an expression of long-standing prejudices and contestation over white identity in the UK", London School of Economics and Political Science, September 29, 2016,
http://blogs.lse.ac.uk/brexit/2016/09/29/post-brexit-hate-crimes-against-poles-are-an-expression-of-long-standing-prejudices-and-contestation-over-white-identity-in-the-uk.

[2] Churchill quoted in Jonathan Walker, *Poland Alone, Britain, SOE and the Collapse of the Polish Resistance*, 1944, History Press, 2008.

[3] Adam Zamoyski and John Murray, *The Forgotten Few, The Polish Air Force in the Second World War*, 1995, p. 8.

[4] Patrick Bishop, *Bomber Boys*, Harper Perennial, London, 2007, p. 56.

[5] Jozef Garlinski, *Poland, SOE and the Allies*, George Allen and Unwin, London, 1969, pg.87. On secret flights by Polish crews from Britain to drop agents into Poland navigators evidently continued to captain their RAF aircraft.

[6] Telephone conversation with Mrs M. Goddard, Polish Enquiries section, RAF, July 24, 2011.

[7] Evan McGilvray, *A Military Government in Exile. The Polish Government-in-Exile 1939-1945, a Study of Discontent*, Helion, 2010. pp. 60-61.

[8] Adrian Carton de Wiart, *Happy Odyssey. The memoirs of Lieutenant-General Sir Adrian Carton de Wiart*, Pan books, 1955, p 123.

[9] Sue Ryder, *Child of my Love*, Harvill Press, London, 1986, pg. 51

[10] Guy R.Williams, *London in the Country, The Growth of Suburbia*, Hamish Hamilton, 1975, p. 125.

[11] Reed was born in Wimbledon, expelled from 13 schools and was a nephew of the film director Sir Carol Reed. He became well-known after a performance in the 1969 film *Women in Love*, in which he wrestled nude with Alan Bates in front of a log fire. He later played in films like *The Devils* and the 1975 musical film *Tommy*.

[12] Patrick Bishop, *Bomber Boys*, Harper Perennial, 2008. About the Author, interview with Louise Tucker pg. 2" The first six years of my life were spent in rural Kent, the scene of much of my first book, *Fighter Boys*," he told Tucker." The rest of my upbringing was in suburban South London, parts of which were hit by the Blitz … I feel comfortable there and I think that is what lies at the heart of the concept of 'home.'"

[13] Frank Miles and Graeme Cranch, *King's College School: The First 150 Years*, Wimbledon, 1979, p.368. Rosser retired in 1978 after 32 very popular years in the Junior School.

[14] Letter to the author, 8.3.84.

[15] Martha Gellhorn," Week-End at Grimsby", in *The Honeyed Peace, A collection of Stories*, Penguin books, 1958, pp. 57-58, 60.

[16] George Mikes, *How To Be An Alien*, Wingate, London, 1957, pg.8. Mikes advised that" it is better to reconcile yourself to the sorrowful reality … There are certain rules, however, which have to be followed if you want to make yourself as acceptable and civilised as you possibly can. Study these rules and imitate the English. There can only be one result: if you don't succeed in imitating them you become ridiculous; if you do, you become even more ridiculous."

[17] Carton de Wiart, p. 99.

[18] On 9 December, 1941 in Malaya, near the Siam border, all available aircraft had been ordered to make a daylight raid on Singora (where the Japanese Army was invading), in Siam. Squadron Leader Scarf, as leader of the raid, had just taken off from the base at Butterworth when enemy aircraft swept in destroying or disabling all the rest of the machines.

The Squadron Leader decided nevertheless to fly alone to Singora. Despite attacks from roving fighters he completed his bombing run and was on his way back when his aircraft became riddled with bullets and he was severely wounded, his left arm had been shattered, he had a large hole in his back and was drifting in and out of consciousness. He managed to crash-land the Blenheim at Alor Star, without causing any injury to his crew, and was rushed to hospital where he died two hours later.

Among those attending him was his wife, a nurse, who gave him blood in a transfusion as part of efforts to save his life.

[19] Adam Zamoyski," Obituary: Lt-Gen Klemns Rudnicki," *The Independent*, Aug. 13, 1992

[20] Douglas Hall, *Art in Exile. Polish Painters in Post-war Britain*, Sansom & Company, Bristol, 2008, p. 34.

[21] Witold Gombrowicz, *Diary, Volume One*, Northwestern University Press, 1988, p. 122.

[22] P.R. Reid, *The Latter Days at Colditz*, Coronet Books, 1965, pg. 15.

[23] Jocelyn Baines, *Joseph Conrad, A critical biography*, Pelican books, 1971, p. 197.

[24] M.R.D. Foot, *SOE, The Special Operations Executive, 1940-1946*, Greenwood Press, 1984p. 241.

[25] Zamoyski, p. 34.

[26] Adam Broner, *My War against the Nazis*, Fire Ant Books, 2007, pg. 97.

[27] Airey Neave, *Saturday at M.I.9*, Coronet, 1974, p. 57.

[28] James W. Blackwell," The Polish Home Army and the struggle for the Lublin region" PHD thesis, University of Glasgow, 2010, p. 2.

[29] Mikes, p. 82.

[30] Jozef Garlinski, *The Survival of Love, Memoirs of a Resistance Officer*, Blackwell, 1991, pp.160-161.

[31] Jan Karski, *Story of a Secret State*, Hodder & Stoughton, London, 1945, pp. 63-64.

[32] Ibid., pp. 197-198.

[33] Richard C. Lukas, *Forgotten Holocaust, The Poles under German Occupation, 1939-1944*, Hippocrene Books, revised edition 2010, p. 13.

[34] Ryder, p. 388.

[35] John Le Carré, *Looking Glass War*, Heinemann, 1965, p. 79.

[36] Karski, p. 231.

[37] Zamoyski, p. 216.

[38] Kratochwil quoted in Hall.

[39] Author email correspondence with Anna Spake, 2013.

[40] Roger Scruton, England: An Elegy, Coninuum Press, 2006. p. 32.

[41] Mikes, p.38.

[42] Madeleine Masson, *Christine: SOE Agent and Churchill's Favourite Spy: A Search for Christine Granville*, Virago, 2005.

[43] Neal Ascherson, *Black Sea*, Vintage, 1996, p. 147.

[44] Page, Leitch, Knightley, *Philby: The Spy who Betrayed a Generation*, Andre Deutsch, 1968, p. 15.

[45] Le Carré, p. 118.

[46] Anthony Powell, *The Military Philosophers*, Fontana, 1977, p. 112.

[47] Len Deighton *Hope*, Harper Paperbacks, 1996, p. 3.

[48] Ted Allbeury, *The Judas Factor*, New English Library, 1985. pp. 5-8.

[49] A. Levin, *The Baltic States*, Yale University Press, Introduction.

[50] Ted Allbeury, *The Special Collection*, Mayflower, 1975, p. 52.

[51] George Steiner, *Anno Domini*, Faber and Faber, 1964, pp. 192-196.

[52] Rebecca West, *The Meaning of Treason*, Penguin, 1965.

[53] Ivo Andric, *The Days of the Consuls*, Dereta, Belgrade, 2000, p. 390.

[54] Desmond O'Grady, *The Turned Card*, Dove, 1995, p. 4.

[55] "Captain Charles Ridley, Obituary," *The Times*, Dec. 15, 2011.

[56] James Buchan, *A Parish of Rich Women*, Penguin Books, 1985.

[57] Robert Graves, *Goodbye to All That*, Penguin, 1960, p. 101.

[58] Anne Blundy, *The Bad News Bible*, Headline, 2004.

[59] Buchan.

[60] For a discussion of Mickiewicz'spoem see Ascherson, p. 161.

[61] Alan Williams, *Barbouze*, Panther, 1975.

[62] Donald Davie, *Collected Poems*, Carcanet Press, 1983,p. 124.

[63] Nicholas Rankin, *Telegram from Guernica*, Faber and Faber, 2003, pp. 146-147.

[64] Norman Sherry, *Conrad and His World*, Thames and Hudson, 1988, p. 102.

[65] Richard Milne," UK finally makes amends for Poland's 60 years of hurt," *Financial Times*, Sept. 5, 2003.

[66] Patrick Bishop, *A Good War*, Hodder Paperbacks, 2008.

[67] Slobodan G. Markovich," British perceptions of Serbia and the Balkans 1903-1906," Dialogue Association, Paris, 2000.

[68] Nick Squires," Secret British agent identified after 65 years," *Daily Telegraph*, June 9, 2009.

[69] Gaby Rado, Television reporter who won three awards from Amnesty International, Obituaries, *The Times*, March 31, 2003.

[70] Eric Ambler, *Light of Day*, William Heinemann, 1962.

[71] Rankin.

[72] Alan Furst, *The Polish Officer*, HarperCollins, 1998.

[73] Leon Uris, *Exodus*, Corgi, 1958.

[74] General Alberto Rovighi," Due paesi con molte cose in commune," Italia E Polonia.

[75] Eric Ambler, *Uncommon Danger*, Fontana, 1983.

[76] Quoted in Desmond O'Grady, *The Turned Card*, Gracewing, 1995.

[77] Eric Linklater, *White-Maa's Saga*, Penguin, 1969, p. 27.

[78] Quoted in George D. Painter, *Marcel Proust, A biography, Vol. 1*, Chatto & Windus, 1965, p. 316.

[79] Paula Fox, *The Coldest Winter, A stringer in liberated Europe*, Henry Holt, 2005, p. 94.

[80] Ewa Lipniacka, *Xenophobe's guide to the Poles*, Oval Books, London, 2009.

[81] Gombrowicz, p. 47.

[82] Michel Gara, "La Pologne a décidé d'ouvrir les dossiers de la police politique," Le Monde, Feb. 13, 2001.

[83] Blackwell, p. 140.

[84] Blackwell, p. 98.

[85] Ian Goldin, Geoffrey Cameron and Meera Balarajan, *Exceptional People*, Princeton University Press, 2011.